CAMBRIDGE LIBRARY COLLECTION

Books of enduring scholarly value

Archaeology

The discovery of material remains from the recent or the ancient past has always been a source of fascination, but the development of archaeology as an academic discipline which interpreted such finds is relatively recent. It was the work of Winckelmann at Pompeii in the 1760s which first revealed the potential of systematic excavation to scholars and the wider public. Pioneering figures of the nineteenth century such as Schliemann, Layard and Petrie transformed archaeology from a search for ancient artifacts, by means as crude as using gunpowder to break into a tomb, to a science which drew from a wide range of disciplines - ancient languages and literature, geology, chemistry, social history - to increase our understanding of human life and society in the remote past.

The XXII Egyptian Royal Dynasty

Karl Richard Lepsius (1810–1884) was a pioneering Prussian Egyptologist considered one of the founders of modern Egyptology. He was commissioned to lead an archaeological expedition to Egypt by the Prussian King Frederick Wilhelm IV in 1842. This 1858 English translation presents an 1856 publication that contained one of the first detailed discussions of the obscure 22nd Dynasty of ancient Egyptian kings. The 22nd Dynasty were descendants of Libyan settlers who ruled between c.943 and 716 BCE in the Third Intermediate Period of Egyptian history, a period characterised by episodes of political instability. Lepsius discusses the chronology of succession in the 22nd Dynasty with reference to texts uncovered by himself and the French archaeologist Auguste Mariette. Although some of Lepsius' assertions regarding the origin of the 22nd Dynasty are now known to be incorrect, his book is still a valuable account of the early historiography of the 22nd Dynasty.

The XXII Egyptian Royal Dynasty

With Some Remarks on XXVI, and Other Dynasties of the New Kingdom

Carl Richard Lepsius

CAMBRIDGE UNIVERSITY PRESS

Cambridge, New York, Melbourne, Madrid, Cape Town, Singapore,
São Paolo, Delhi, Dubai, Tokyo

Published in the United States of America by Cambridge University Press, New York

www.cambridge.org
Information on this title: www.cambridge.org/9781108017398

This edition first published 1858
This digitally printed version 2010

ISBN 978-1-108-01739-8 Paperback

THE

XXII. EGYPTIAN ROYAL DYNASTY,

WITH

SOME REMARKS ON XXVI. AND OTHER DYNASTIES OF THE NEW KINGDOM.

BY

DR. RICHARD LEPSIUS,

PROFESSOR OF THE UNIVERSITY AT BERLIN.

TRANSLATED BY

WILLIAM BELL, ESQ., PHIL. DR.

HONORARY SECRETARY OF THE CHRONOLOGICAL INSTITUTE, AND MEMBER OF VARIOUS FOREIGN AND ENGLISH SOCIETIES, AUTHOR OF "STREAM OF TIME," "SHAKSPERE'S PUCK," &c., &c.

WITH TWO LITHOGRAPHIC PLATES OF GENEALOGIES, TRANSLATED AND SUPERINTENDED BY PROFESSOR LEPSIUS AT BERLIN; BY WHOM ALSO THE METAL TYPES IN THE BODY OF THE WORK USED BY HIMSELF FOR THE ORIGINAL WERE FURNISHED.

LONDON:

PRINTED FOR THE AUTHOR, 31, BURTON STREET, BURTON CRESCENT.

SOLD BY

MESSRS. TRÜBNER AND CO., 60, PATERNOSTER ROW;

AND ALL BOOKSELLERS.

1858.

Price 10*s*. 6*d*.

LONDON:
J. HADDON, PRINTER, CASTLE STREET, FINSBURY.

PREFACE.

SOME friends, feeling interest in the latest discussion on the wonderful revelations exhumed from the Egyptian soil generally, but more especially from the Grave Chambers of Saqâra, requested from me an exact Translation of the most recent publication of the well-known Egyptologist, Professor Dr. Richard Lepsius, of Berlin. I assented to their wishes, and the result is contained in the following pages, which I should scarcely have ventured on had not Professor Lepsius himself kindly assented to the work, and, besides giving me his latest correction on one or two points, had he not also done me the great favour of securing, from the Royal Berlin Foundry, the metal hieroglyphical types used by himself, as of unsurpassed beauty, as well as in translating and superintending, in lithography, the two plates of Genealogies in hieroglyphics appended to the work: for all this I beg, publicly, to return him my best thanks. As the first instance of the use of metal hieroglyphical types in this country, the present publication may serve for an era in the typographical art; and I may return also my thanks to Mr. John Haddon, the printer, and to Mr. Williams, his overseer, for the accuracy in their use, which, in so new and difficult arrangement, naturally required great attention, and presented many composing difficulties, happily, I trust, and successfully overcome.

WILLIAM BELL. PHIL. DR.

31, Burton Street, Burton Crescent, W.C.
London, St. George's Day, 1858.

PROFESSOR DR. RICHARD LEPSIUS

ON THE

XXII. EGYPTIAN ROYAL DYNASTY, &c.

HAVING previously laid before the Academy the reconstruction of the XII. Manethonic Dynasty of the old Egyptian Kingdom, and afterwards the completion of the Ptolemaic Dynasty according to the monuments, I now turn my attention to one of the most important dynasties of the new Pharaonic rule—the XXII. of Manetho, which governed in the 10th and 9th centuries before Christ, and to which King *Šišaq*, a contemporary of Rheoboam, and conqueror of Jerusalem, belongs.

The first promise of the young government—which, springing up after the mighty struggle of the war against the Hyksos, began under the XVII. Dynasty, strengthened itself under Tuthmosis and Amenophis of the XVIII., reached with Sethos and Ramses of the XIX. its highest development, but towards the end of this same dynasty was already exhausted—had, under the Ramesides of the XX. Dynasty, through luxury, sloth, and the continued increase of the priestly power, gradually given way to an internal dissolution; and to which the royal Theban races, at the end of the XX. Dynasty, fell a sacrifice. A man of Tanis, a native of the eastern boundary of the Delta, *Herhor*, had raised himself, under the last of the Rameses, to the dignity of "First Prophet of Ammon-Ra," and took at the same time the title [hieroglyphs] "Illustrious of Upper and Lower Egypt," and [hieroglyphs] "Prince of *Kus*," which appear to have denoted the highest administrative offices of the entire kingdom. After this king's death, of whose offspring nothing is known, *Herhor* caused himself to be crowned[1] king *de facto*, took on him all the royal titles of his predecessors, and thus founded a new dynasty. He retained therefore, when king, his office of High Priest of Ammon, and assumed even this title in his first royal cartouche. In his second shield he added to his former name that of a son of Ammon, *Siamun;* as did later Alexander the Great, who also, after the conquest of Egypt, let himself be called in his hieroglyphical shield, *Siamun Alexander*, as this one *Siamun Herhor*. But under the successors of Herhor there are many who unite the dignity of high priest with the royal title; and when the king laid down the pontiff dignity it was only to transfer

B

it to his successor; so that thus the highest office of the Egyptian hierarchy was always combined in the closest manner with the crown.

The same relations were continued in the XXII. Dynasty, in which we too generally find the eldest son appearing on the monuments at first as High Priest of Ammon-Ra; sometimes conjoined with his royal father, but sometimes alone. This dynasty, therefore, with which we are here principally concerned, kept substantially its character as a pontiff dynasty. It is called by Manetho a *Bubastic* one; this means that its head, *Šešonk I.*, had his origin in the town of Bubastis, which lay north of Tanis, the birth-place of the founder of the XXI. Dynasty, which, like the other, was situated on one of the eastern arms of the Nile. The modern ruins of *Tel Basta* represent the site of the ancient Bubastis, which was in the neighbourhood of the Biblical *Goshen;* if indeed it did not belong to it. According to Herodotus, it was at Bubastis that the famed canal was drawn off from the Nile, which was carried by Ramses-Sesostris only eastward to the Low Plains of the Desert, afterwards by Neko to the Bitter Lakes, but taken by Darius into the Red Sea; and thus became the first junction canal betwixt the Red and Mediterranean Seas. It is well known that it was on this Ramses Canal that the Israelites were forced to build the towns Pithom (Patumos of Herodotus) and Ramses, so called from its founder, Ramses II.; after they doubtless had been compelled to the same hard serfdom on the canal which necessitated the building of those cities. We may therefore fancy that country immediately adjacent to the Arabian Desert as principally inhabited by a Semitic people and its descendants; and this explains to us the abnormal, un-Egyptian character in the royal names of this Bubastic Dynasty, which has been already frequently remarked by other parties, and to which we shall subsequently recur. We have now to do with a royal race of Semitic origin, which therefore may have been related to, and possibly were, the descendants of those harassed and expelled Israelites, that doubtless had settled for the greater part in Bubastis, the principal town of that neighbourhood. The conqueror of Jerusalem sprung from a Semitic family in Bubastis.

We have a pretty large number of monuments of this Dynasty. Isolated sculptures, and similar objects, formed portions of the first Egyptian collections brought to Europe. Champollion, as early as 1824, recognised in his first application of his great discovery of the royal names in his "*Précis du Système hiéroglyphique*," two of the new kings of this Dynasty, *Šešonk* and an *Osarkon*, the Σέσωνχις and Ὀσορχών of the Manetho List. In Turin, in 1826,[2] he found the third dynastic name of this Dynasty, *Takelot*, Τακέλωθις of Manetho, on the fragment of a wooden stele, the other portion of which is in Rome. In Egypt it is principally on a portion of the large metropolitan temple of Karnak that representations of this Dynasty have been preserved. It seems that the first court of this temple was erected by the Bubastides, or at least begun by them. The plan of this court has this irregularity, that a separate smaller temple breaks through the circuit of the south wall, and projects with its front into the court. This irregularity is explained from the circumstance that this smaller temple, built by Ramses of the XX. Dynasty, was already existing when the plan for this court was determined on. Who completed the work cannot now be ascertained, because the walls are devoid of sculpture, with the exception of the angle betwixt the present second Pylon, on which this court abuts, and the before-mentioned temple, built by Ramses III. This interposed building, which also forms an outlet on the south side of the court, as well as the outer south side of the large temple, to the left of any one going out, is completely covered with figures and inscriptions of the kings of the XXII. Dynasty; and on this south side we find the well-known representation of 156 prisoners conducted by Ammon to King *Šešonk,* amongst whom the king of Judæa is introduced. In the interior of the court Wilkinson found, besides the three kings known to Champollion, also a second *Šešonk* and a second *Osarkon;* so that he could ascribe, in his "*Materia Hieroglyphica*" (1828), five monarchs to this Dynasty, and bring them into the present true series. The French-Tuscan expedition carried our knowledge no farther. Rosellini,[3] who gave in the text of his great work a *résumé* of the historical results of the expedition, gives the five kings, which Wilkinson had already arranged, and in a better sequence. But Leemans, in his Letter to Salvolini (1838, p. 109, *seq.*) attempted to point out the entire Manethonic Dynasty on the monuments. He used many monuments from different museums, that had not been previously taken into consideration for this purpose; particularly the letters of a statue of the Nile in the British Museum, in which the names of a King Osarchon and of his son Scheschonk, with the name of the maternal grandsire of the latter, are contained. He put this Osarkon in the fourth place of the Dynasty, as Osarkon II., and his son as Scheschonk III., in the fifth place He found also a second Takelot on some Leyden funeral urns, and a fourth Osarkon upon a seal-stone in the same collection.

The series, however, of the XXII. Dynasty was not completely distinguishable from that of the XXI. and XXIII., between which it was interposed; both of them sprung from the town of Tanis, a neighbour of Bubastis. Both these dynasties might be then said to have been almost entirely untouched. Champollion has certainly placed two kings of the XXI. Dynasty, which he read *Manduftep* and *Aasen,* and ascribed them to the *Smendes* and *Psusennes* of Manetho. Both hieroglyphical names, of which the latter appears only a private name, belong to the old kingdom. Rosellini followed Champollion's idea; not so Wilkinson, who omitted them, and Leemans gave them their proper places. As, however, no other names were put in lieu of them, the XXI. and XXIII. Dynasties continued void.

My restoration of these three Dynasties connectively, as I attempted in my "Egyptian Travels," according to the materials then accessible, was published in 1845[4] in Bunsen's work, as I communicated it to him for that purpose. The three monumental names that I ascribed to the XXI. Dynasty, as well as the other three of the XXIII., may be taken as so far established. But still it has been truly remarked, and I think first by De Rougé, that the high-priest *Pianχ*, the father of *Pisem*,[5] is not met with as king; his apposition, therefore, for Manetho's *Psinaches* must be very doubtful. I have further satisfied myself in Thebes that the king *Siamun Herhor* (read formerly Pehor) appears already at the end of the XXII. Dynasty as a private name,[6] and cannot, therefore (as I formerly thought possible), stand for the 'Οσοχώρ of the lists, but belongs to the commencement of the dynasty.

The series of the kings of the XXII. Dynasty hitherto known, as given in Bunsen's work, has not since been altered. But as I could not previously take but few ascertained points from then existing materials, and had to settle the remainder from probabilities, so now many important monuments have since turned up, which permit an essentially improved restoration of this dynasty. We are indebted for these new lights principally to the very rich and important discoveries made by M. Mariette in the Apis sepulchres.

But while, unfortunately, no Apis of the XXI. or XXIII. Dynasties has been found, seven of them fall within the XXII. Dynasty. The years of their decease are noted during the reigns of five out of its nine kings, and of these five, two were previously entirely unknown. The most important of them for our restoration is one noted by M. Mariette as 1959. This was fixed by a priest of Neith, *Horpeson* (or *Pesonhor?*) in the year of the death of the seventh Apis, in the 37th year of the last of these nine monarchs, *Šešonk IV.;* whose cartouches have been first discovered by M. Mariette. It contains in its upper division the worship of Horpeson before the holy Apis Bull; in its lower one the relation of the year of the birth of this Apis, its enthronization or introduction into the Temple of Hephaistos at Memphis, and of its death, with a long genealogy of the sacrificer. He mentions not less than fifteen generations of ancestry, and comprehends in them not only the time of the rule of the entire dynasty, at the end of which he lived, but ascends even six generations higher. As far as the eleventh of these generations he adduces fathers and mothers, but after that only fathers. The circumstance most important to us, as no doubt also to the erector, is that in the sixth degree his descent from a king of the reigning family is given, and that from this king upwards the earlier kings are mentioned to the founder of the dynasty; and that the six earliest links also show us the private ancestors of the Bubastidian royal family, which carry us back to about the extinction of the Theban royal house, and the origin of Herhor, the head of the XXI. Dynasty, which took its rise at Tanis.

Mariette adduces, in his important essays on the Apis graves, this stele,[7] naturally for his revision of the XXII. Dynasty; but he mistakes the unbroken upward series of genealogies in it. He takes only the first cartouche, which exhibits the title neb toni, as a royal one; the three others he considers as the names of princes, as the preceding group "royal son," as the proper title, instead of letting this cartouche-name belong to it as genitive of the father's name. He gets thereby three different breaks, and lets the gifts of Apis be supplicated, not only for the Priest Horpeson, but also for the three princes, and for their god-like father, Namurot. If the inscription were to be thus construed, all these persons would have to have been represented with the princes in the van, and these breaks would have been more strictly defined.[8] Finally, it would be contrary to a rule which admits few exceptions to put the names of princes in royal cartouches, and the more so, as the same stele contains the name of an ascertained prince and princess, without the Rings.

M. Mariette has possibly been induced to refrain from the natural explanation of the inscription from the circumstance that the first shield of the kings does not stand before the following ones. In inscriptions like the present this has no difficulty whatsoever, and M. Mariette adduces on the same page a king's shield from another Apis-stele, on which "Son of the (king) *Peχi*" is written without other royal sign but the cartouche;[9] and this is the case also on later Apis-stelæ and elsewhere. The true meaning of the four shield-names is hereby finally put beyond doubt, since the mothers of these four kings have the title "god-like mother," a title especially given to the mother of a king, who was not queen, but the subordinate wife (*Nebenfrau*) of the regal father, or the wife of a private person whose son was raised to be king. In an analogous method, the non-regal father of a king, as here Namurot, the father of the first king, gets the title "god-like father." Cases like this frequently occur in the XIII. Dynasty of Manetho, as well as later down to the Ptolemies. But some irregularities of the inscription fall to the share of the writer. For instance, the group "son of" is four times wanting before the name of the mother; this was certainly, taken strictly, not necessary, since the denoting of the son before the father's name might suffice both for father and mother: once, however, the sign of "son" is wanting, where it on no account ought to be so; and once there stands "royal son," where "son" solely ought to be. This error is plainly apparent, since both parents are private persons.[10] The writer had, in transcribing the genealogy, clearly made the mistake of a line, for at his father, the sign for "royal" where it was to be expected, is wanting. Strange, finally, is it that by the sign "royal mother," is denoted the grandmother of the first king in the genealogy.

Here, certainly, we might more readily suppose a case which would justify this denotation;[10*] perhaps the writer ought to have put  "royal daughter," instead of  "royal mother," the Goose instead of the Vulture, and was thereto led by the nine previous titles of the Vulture  to repeat it here again.

After these remarks the text of the inscription may be assuredly corrected and given synoptically, as follows :—

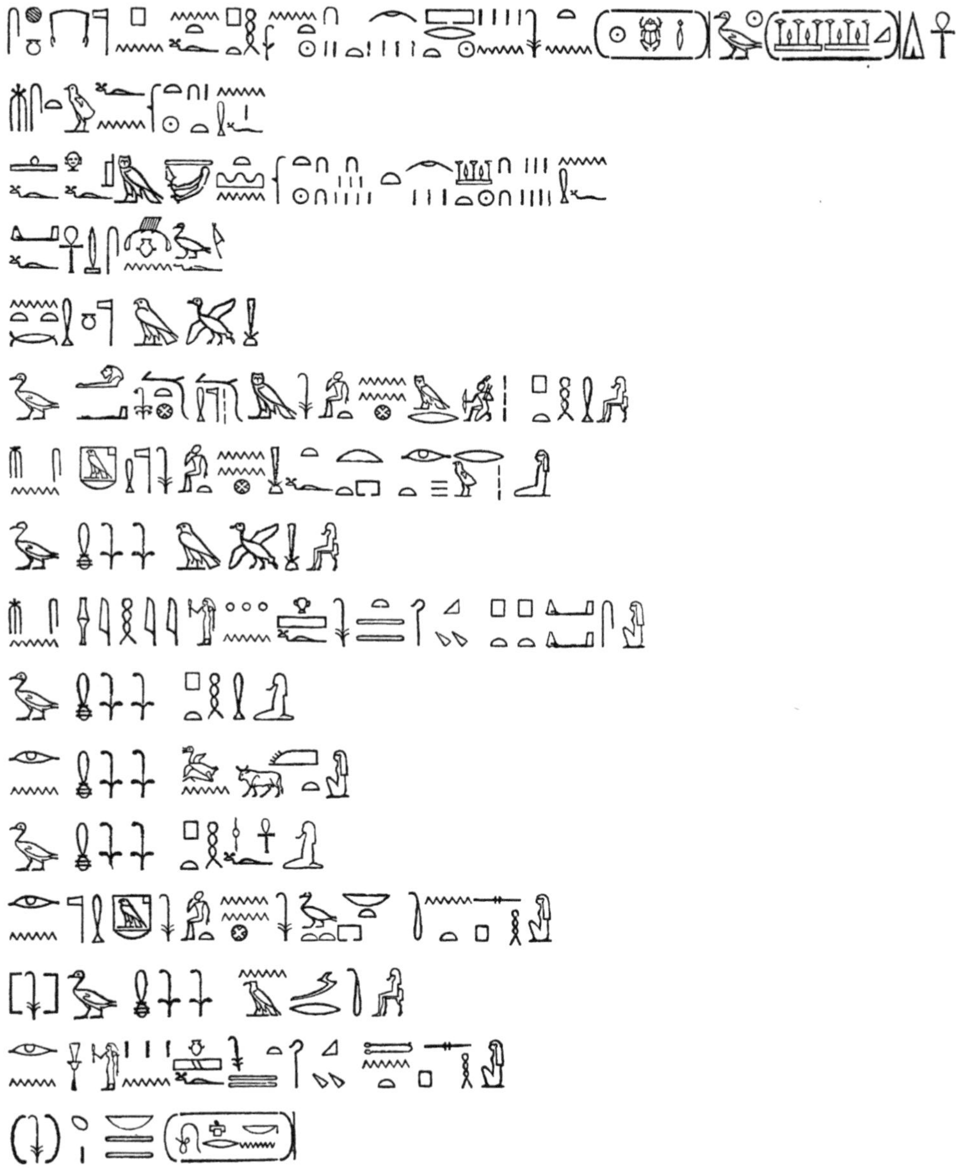

The sign [ ] in square brackets is to be rejected; the groups in round brackets must be supplied, and then we gain the whole in the following genealogical form :—

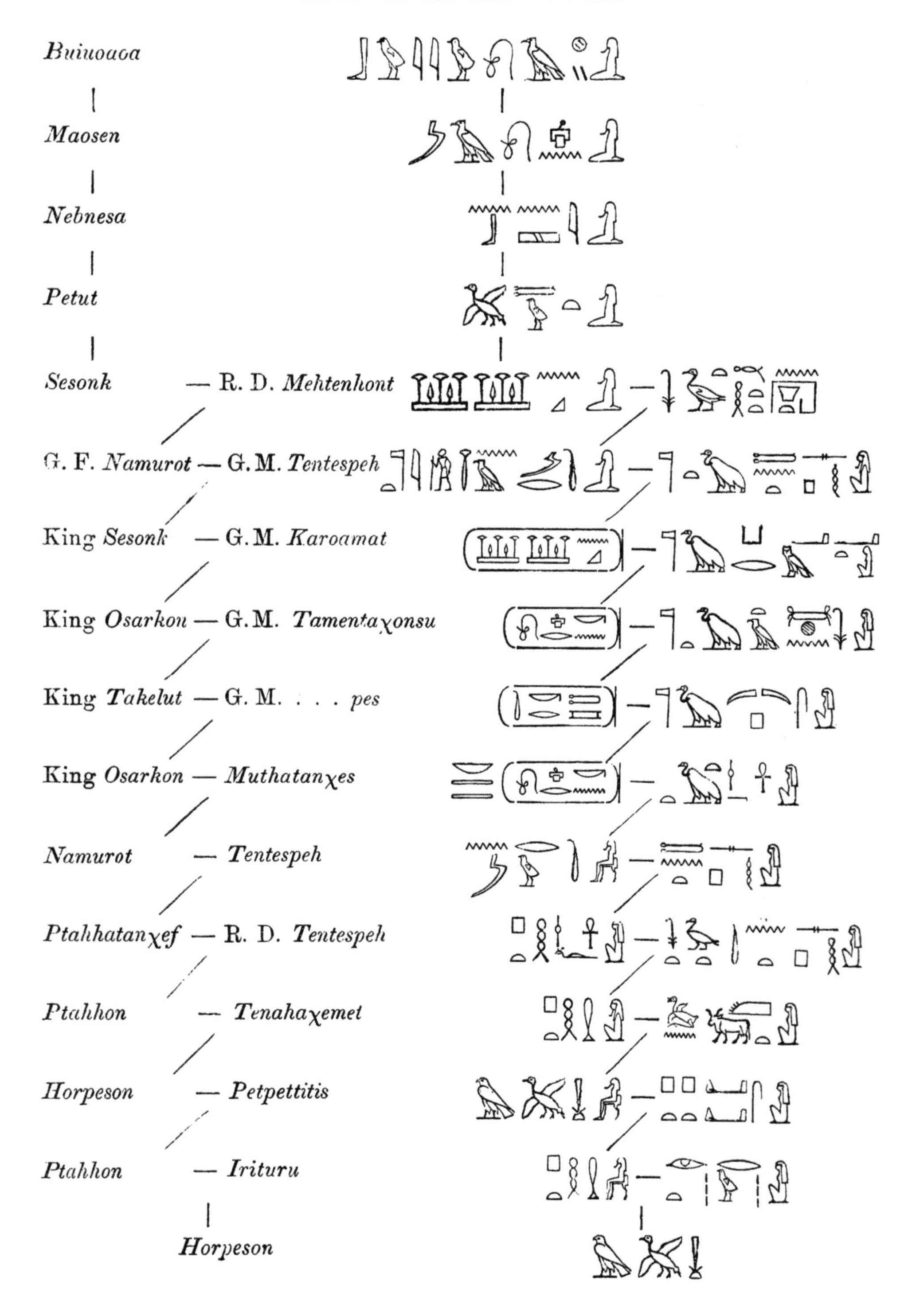
Buiuoaoa
Maosen
Nebnesa
Petut
Sesonk — R. D. Mehtenhont
G. F. Namurot — G. M. Tentespeh
King Sesonk — G. M. Karoamat
King Osarkon — G. M. Tamentaχonsu
King Takelut — G. M. . . . pes
King Osarkon — Muthatanχes
Namurot — Tentespeh
Ptahhatanχef — R. D. Tentespeh
Ptahhon — Tenahaχemet
Horpeson — Petpettitis
Ptahhon — Irituru
Horpeson

If (and we cannot assume it otherwise) the king *Šešonk*, from whose 37th year the inscription is dated, belonged to the XXII. Dynasty, nor is the name found in any other dynasty, it is evident that he belongs to the end, and his four royal ancestors to the beginning of this dynasty, which had, according to Manetho's Lists, nine kings; the first of these four named kings is the ninth forefather of the priest *Horpeson*. The number of these generations, therefore, shows that the inscription names the four first and the last kings of this dynasty. That the first of these four must have begun a dynasty is shown incontestibly thereby that his parents here named were private persons; and it is perfectly in accordance with Manetho's Tables that the first name here, as in the Lists, is a *Šešonk*.

These Lists give us only three names in this dynasty. According to Eusebius, these three would comprise the entire dynasty, but Africanus, on the contrary, gives them with greater exactness as,

I.	Σέσωγχις	governs	21	years.
II.	Ὀσορθών	„	15	„
III—V.	Ἄλλοι τρεῖς	„	25	„
VI.	Τακέλλωθις	„	13	„
VII—IX.	Ἄλλοι τρεῖς	„	42	„

These, therefore, together rule 120 years.

But the total of the specified years is not 120, but only 116. And also, instead of Ὀσορθών we ought certainly to read Ὀσορχών, as the hieroglyphical orthography *Osarkon*, pronounced in the Memphitic dialect *Osarχon*, proves. This List, therefore, shows that not only the first but also the second name in our inscription agrees with that of Manetho. The third, fourth, and fifth names are wanting in his List; our inscription supplies the two next following places; it gives us *Takelut* and a second *Osarkon* for the third and fourth king of the dynasty. The sixth is given in the List; he was a Takelut, and therefore the second of his name. Under him died an Apis; and the succeeding Apis tombs, whose epochs and successions we know by Mariette's careful investigations upon the spot, give us the names of the three following kings in a settled order, namely, a *Šešonk*, a *Peχi* (till then unknown), and the latest *Šešonk*, from whose 37th year the stele is dated.

There is therefore only the fifth king wanting, whom neither Manetho's List nor the stelæ name. The other monuments now step in. These name four different *Šešonks*, and we have in the List hitherto only three; so that, as the one wanting finds only one place open—the fifth—that must be filled with this *Šešonk*.[11]

Thus the entire dynasty is produced with perfect surety, according to their family names, as follows:—

1. *Šešonk I.*
2. *Osarkon I.*
3. *Takelut I.*
4. *Osarkon II.*
5. *Šešonk II.*
6. *Takelut II.*
7. *Šešonk III.*
8. *Peχi.*
9. *Šešonk IV.*

From this series, in the first instance, an important error in our former adopted List is deducible, since the previous third king, *Hor-Petuχanu,* must be entirely removed, and ascribed to the XXI. The traces of his family connexion with the XXII. Dynasty made it previously specious, notwithstanding a break thereby in the direct succession, that he belonged to this dynasty. This supposition can now be rescinded, and no interruption in the direct succession need be shown.

Since, however, in the above List the same family name occurs three and four times, this List, as it must have stood with Manetho, is not sufficient to distinguish the kings of one name on the monuments. It is well known that each king, in addition to his family name, took at his accession a second shield-name; and we have therefore now to combine the proper throne-names with those of the family shields. As my present order varies from my previous one, I will now distinguish the similar and partly identical names by figures, according with the order of the above table.

Concerning the throne-name of *Šešonk I.* there is no difference of opinion. He is the king whose shields may be read on the south side of the temple of Karnak, in finely carved hieroglyphics. The figure of the king to whom the Asiatic prisoners are conducted by Ammon is only sketched, not finished. In the interior, too, of the portico, his shields are found on the architrave above the columns, where the builder of a new portion, named in the inscription, puts his name. This local situation of his sculptures gives him place before the other kings of this dynasty named there; nor is it possible to assign his shields to the place of the third or fourth *Šešonk,* as their succession is settled by the Apis-stelæ. Were we to place him in lieu of *Šešonk II.* in the fifth place of the dynasty, he must then come after Osarkon I., which the Karnak sculptures prevent. With Manetho's duration of his twenty-one years' reign, it is in conformity that we find on a stele in Selseleh[11*] mention of his XXI. regnant year.

Osarkon I. has also left sculptures in the portico of Karnak, worked with the same elaborate care as those of his predecessor. He has, as little as *Šešonk I.,* a distinguishing cognisance in his family shield, for the adjoined *Miamun* was adopted by all the kings of this dynasty. In contradistinction, however, Osarkon II. was accustomed to assume in his shield the adjunct *Si Bast,* son of the goddess *Bast* (Bubastis), or else *Si Hiset,* son of Isis, by which he shows himself a later Osarkon than the first. We find, further, that on the Apis stelæ the 23rd year of Osarkon II. mentioned; we cannot therefore put him in the place of our first *Osarkon,* because to him Manetho gives expressly only 15 regnant years.[12] Still less possible is it to change him for our Osarkon III., the second king of the XXIII. Dynasty, because the Karnak sculptures preclude that.

The third king of this dynasty, and also the sixth, is named *Takelut,* and the monuments give also two kings of this name.

Amongst the representations at Karnak[13] is one which gives *Takelut II.* before Ammon-Ra. Behind him follows his son, clothed in a tiger's skin, named *Osarkon.* He is described in the attached inscription as "High Priest of Ammon-Ra," and was therefore probably designated successor of his father. Upon another wall[14] of the same place this Prince High Priest of Ammon, *Osarkon,* is represented alone bringing offerings to Ammon-Ra, and then follows a long inscription of the twelfth year of his father, *Takelut.* We have already seen from the Apis stele, No. 1959, that a son Osarkon, the second of his name, follows Takelut I. in the government. Nothing is therefore more probable than to place the Takelut of Karnak as the first, and to consider his son as the later Osarkon II.; and this the sooner, since the second Takelut had no Osarkon for a successor. We must, however, renounce this succession, and accept another, according to which the Takelut of Karnak is the second, and the other, whose throne-shield exists only upon some leathern fragments in Berlin, is the first, on the following grounds. In both representations the Prince Osarkon is named son of our Takelut II. and of the queen *Mimut-Karomama.* But, opposed to this, King Osarkon II. is called on the Apis stele son of a Takelut, by the god-like mother . . . *pes.* It is extremely possible that Takelut, besides his royal spouse, might have had a second wife, but he could not have had from both at once his succeeding son Osarkon; and, as the place of the . . . *pes* by the Apis stele is settled as wife of the *first* Takelut, the queen *Karomama* must have been wife of the *second* Takelut; and a further consequence is, that her son, the high priest *Osarkon* did not reign, since after Takelut II. a *Šešonk* followed. A second reason for forcing us to leave Takelut II. in his place, is that in the opposite case we then must assume an error in the succession of the Apis beasts as settled by Mariette, and in which our Takelut II. must take stand behind, and not before, Osarkon II.

That this *Osarkon II.,* the first-named king in the Apis sepulchres, has the fourth place in this dynasty has been proved before.

This king had a son *Šešonk,* as appears from the inscriptions of a statue found in the Apis cave, and by a second wife, *Karoama.* We have shown above that a *Šešonk* must be put in the place of the fifth king; though this name appears neither in Manetho's Lists nor is found on the Apis stele which has hitherto vouched for the order of these names. We cannot therefore doubt that this Prince *Šešonk,* a son of Osarkon II., succeeded his father as *Šešonk II.* in the government, and the shields belong to him which hitherto, as far as I know, are only found on a scarabæus which I possess in a cast, and which was furnished me by M. Migliarini in Florence.

The latest kings of this dynasty are fixed from the stelæ which mention the fourteenth year of *Takelut II.*, the twenty-ninth of *Šešonk III.*, the second of *Peχi,* and the thirty-seventh of *Šešonk IV.*

For the succession of *Šešonk III.* and *Peχi* is ascertained from three stelæ, on which the birth and enthronization of an Apis is mentioned under the first, and his death under the second. And still surer is the place of *Šešonk IV.* next to *Peχi,* since he is called his son upon the stele No. 1933. And furthermore, that these three kings stand at the end of the dynasty, is evident, as before said, from the number of generations which are reckoned on stele No. 1959, betwixt *Pethiset,* contemporary with King *Šešonk IV.*, and the four first kings of the dynasty. On the other hand, we must, for the rank of *Osarkon II.* and *Takelut II.* depend upon M. Mariette's observations on the locality of the Apis tombs, giving us this succession; should such succession be disturbed, it might indeed be objected that it is possible to confound the first and second Takeluts, if the certainly very doubtful assumption were allowable that [hieroglyphs] the second wife of Takelut, who would thus be the first, was so at the same time with the queen Karomama,that each had had a son Osarkon, and that the son of the subordinate wife had succeeded to the government after that the son of the queen had died before his father. The facts hitherto ascertained give no reason for any other order than what we have stated.

Mariette, in his often-cited papers, puts eleven kings in this dynasty, instead of Manetho's nine; by simply placing in the former rows the two kings newly discovered in the Apis tombs. According to what has been said, only nine kings can be shown for this dynasty, because two kings formerly received into it are now discarded.

On a comparison of the previous order of these shields, as given identically by Bunsen, Lesueur, and Mariette, we find the following conformities and variances. *Šešonk I.* remains. Their second and fourth king represent together our *Osarkon II.* For we have, with the family shield of the *Osarkon,* two throne-shields, of which one reads, *Ra-sesur-ma-sotep-en-Ra,* the other, *Ra-sesur-ma-sotep-en-Amun.* I formerly supposed that both these shields belonged to different *Osarkons*, but the change of such additions as *sotep-en-Ra, sotep-en-Amun*, &c., is too common in the foregoing dynasties that we should object to receive them but as mere variations of the same name.

The third king of the earlier List, *Hor-Petuχanu*, we have already referred to the XXI. Dynasty; we shall have to revert to him again. The fourth king, *Osarkon II.*, remains in position; as well as his successor, *Šešonk II.* The sixth king remains also the same, he was, however, in this earlier List the first, and is now the second of his name. There followed, as seventh king, and third Osarkon, our *Osarkon I.* The result seemed formerly unavoidable, that the Osarkon who appears in Karnak as the High Priest of Ammon-Ra, and son of Takelut II. and his queen, Karomama, followed his father on the throne. Now, King *Peχi* takes his place, and in like manner the former *Takelut*, whose throne-shield was not known, must give place to *Šešonk IV.* Two new kings have stepped in instead of King *Hor-Petuχanu*, and a variation *Osarkon II.*; a third king, namely, the present King *Takelut I.*, who was only formerly surmised, has gotten his throne-shield, and has thereby a settled place in the dynasty.

If we now pass to the separate monuments, in which one or more members of this dynastic family are mentioned, the easy settlement of their succession in the series, as we have placed them, is an important confirmation of its correctness.

The genealogical Apis stele from which we set out, names the four first kings of the dynasty, to each of whom we have added their throne-shields. It is remarkable that not only the first (which could not be otherwise) but also the three following kings had no queens for mothers, as proved by the four-times repeated title, "heavenly mother."

Besides the here-named subordinate wife of the third king, Takelut I., we gain knowledge of a second, who also did not bear the royal titles. Of the fourth king, Osarkon II., the monuments name even three subordinate wives, without a queen. It is only of the sixth king, Takelut II., that the queen, *Mimut-Karomama*, appears as "*himet suten uert*," "high, royal wife," where the addition, "high," at the same time, perhaps, designates the head-wife; but we know, besides her, a second wife of the same king. It is apparent from this that the Pharaohs of this period, like David and his successors, had many subordinate wives; and also that they, as well as the queens, could have sons capable of the succession.

The Apis stele, No. 1898, which is dated from the 28th year of King *Šešonk III.*, was placed by an officer, *Pethiset* (*Petisis*), and his two sons. This Petisis was son of the officer *Takelut*, and of the Princess[15] *Tesbastperu*; but *Takelut*, son of Prince *Šešonk*, whose father is stated as King *Osarkon II.* This king is named in the upper part of the stele only by his family name, *Miamun-Osarkon*, but in the lower inscription only with his throne-shield, *Rasesur-ma-sotep-*

en-Amun; but the repetition of the same person allows no doubt on the subject, that both shields belong together: from this the identity with Osarkon II. is deduced. The genealogy of this stele is therefore as follows :—

King *Osarkon II.*

|

Prince *Šešonk*

|

Officer *Takelut* — Princess *Tesbastperu*

Officer *Pethiset* — *Tari.*

Hence Petisis descends in the fourth degree from King *Osarkon II.*, as also does King *Šešonk III.*, under whom the stele was placed. The two middle links are called *Šešonk* and *Takelut* in the royal family, as well as that of Petisis. Mariette takes the prince *Šešonk* for the same as King *Šešonk II.*, the successor of *Osarkon II.* But then again he supposed (pp. 90, 94) that after *Šešonk II.*, the crown did not descend to the son, but passed to a foreign, or, at least, not documentedly related, branch who took to wife a niece of *Šešonk II.*, grand-daughter of *Osarkon II.*, namely, the *Karomama* mentioned as queen.[16] Hereby the direct succession, and, according to customary dynastic rules, the dynasty itself, would have finished. But there is no reason why we should not follow the natural presumption that King *Takelut* is one and the same with that *Takelut* noted on the stele as an officer, son of the prince and subsequent king, *Šešonk II.* For there is no doubt that King Takelut II. had, at the same time, or in succession, besides his aunt Tesbastperu, whom alone Mariette allows him, also his cousin, Karomama, to wife. It is a more difficult question, whence comes it that in an inscription under *Šešonk III.*, his great great grandfather, King Osarkon II., bears behind his shield the addition [hieroglyphs] which, in general, only living kings use; and that the two royal predecessors of *Šešonk III.*, namely, *Šešonk II.* and *Takelut II.*, are not adduced as kings, but the first as prince, the last as officer? The best supposition seems to be that King *Osarkon II.*, besides his successor, *Šešonk II.*, had another son, *Šešonk*, the father of Takelut, and grandfather of Petisis; and this need not be cast aside as impossible. On further consideration, namely, of the lifetimes which are presupposed in the above data, the case here taken as possible appears to me as the most probable, viz., that *Osarkon II.* had two sons of the name of *Šešonk.* The grandfather of Petisis would then have been the eldest, and died, perhaps, before the birth of the second *Šešonk II.* With them we gain two new links in the genealogy of this family, which now forms itself as represented on Lithograph Plate I.; differing from the German impressions of 1856.* But it is also possible, and this case is here taken as the

* Communicated in a Letter from Professor Lepsius, July, 1857, to the Translator; with the corrected and beautiful Lithographs at the end of this Book.—[NOTE BY THE TRANSLATOR.]

more probable of the two, that *Šešonk II.*, whilst prince, had the future *Takelut II.* as his son; and that Petisis was born whilst this Takelut was still merely officer. He who prefers the former assumption, on which I will not definitively decide, cannot strike out Takelut, father of Petisis, singly from the royal series, but must also hold the Prince *Šešonk*, whom Mariette considers as the subsequent king, for a brother of King *Šešonk II.*, of the same name. The posterity of Petisis, who, from the stele already mentioned, and two others, Nos. 1904 and 1905, from the second year of King *Peχi* had three wives, are drawn on the accompanying lithographic table.[17]

Upon a statue, too, which Mariette found in the Apis tombs, his son is called Prince *Šešonk.*

Osarkon II. — *Karoamat*

|

Prince *Šešonk.*

And here the name of his mother, *Karoamat,* is superadded. She does not appear as queen, according to Mariette's erroneous assertion, but without further addition; and we therefore may consider her only as a subordinate wife.

On the already discussed stele, No. 1959, we find a subordinate wife of *Osarkon II.* already named, different from this, the mother of Namurot.[18] We find also a third subordinate wife of Osarkon II. on four alabaster vases of Mr. Campion, in Cahira;[19] from which we gain the following genealogy:—

King *Osarkon si-bast* — *Hiset-en-χeb*

|

Princess *Tesbastperu.*

The throne-shield of the king is certainly wanting, and it is therefore uncertain with which Osarkon we here have to do. But the addition *Si-bast,* "Son of Bubastis," points to the second Osarkon; since no such addition is known for the former. And, moreover, that we now know the princess *Tesbastperu* for the wife of Takelut II.; otherwise we must admit two princesses of the same name, if here Osarkon I. was the person in question.

We find in Karnak, amongst the sculptures of the XXII. Dynasty, many above-mentioned representations of a prince and high-priest *Osarkon,* son of Takelut II. and of the queen *Karomama,* who is called the daughter of a high-priest *Namurot,* son of the king *Osarkon si-bast.* We thereby gain the following series:—

King *Osarkon si-bast*

|

High Priest *Namurot*

|

Queen *Mimut Karomama* — King *Takleut II.*

|

High Priest *Osarkon.*

There can be no doubt upon any link here but the first, since the throne-shield of this King Osarkon is wanting. He is, however, known beyond a doubt for *Osarkon II.*, first from the addition, *Si-bast,* and secondly from his relationship to *Takelut II.*

Upon a wooden coloured stele, of which the one half is at Turin, the other at Rome,[20] a priest (or high-priest) of Ammon is pictured bringing offerings to the Sun-God, Ra; who is called prince of the King *Takelut,* and son of *Tašpu,* the daughter of *Ḥor-minuter.* From this follows the following relationships.

Ḥor-minuter
|
King *Takelut* — *Tašpu*
|
Prince *Namurot.*

Since King Takelut here is mentioned without any addition, it is a probability, but nothing more, that *Takelut I.* is here intended; and this probability is increased, since we know already that Takelut II. had two wives.

A fragmentary statue in the possession of Dr. John Lee, of Hartwell House, Bucks, published by Mr. S. Sharpe,[21] gives a "royal grandson,"[22] *Muntuhotep,* whose wife was granddaughter of a King Takelut. The entire connexion which results from these different tables is the following:—

King *Takelut*
|
Prince *Tet-Ptah Aufanχ Amunnebkettotti* — Roy. Daughter *Anχkaroamat*
| |
Taχat — Royal Grandson *Muntuhotep*
|
Tet-Ptah Aufanχ.

Here, too, King *Takelut* is named without addition, and may be referred to either of the Takeluts. The princess *Anχkaroamat* may, on the most reasonable grounds, be assumed as a daughter of King Takelut, being in equal degree with Prince Tetptah-Aufanχ. We have taken him for King Takelut II. without being able to assign any special reason for or against. The choice remains, therefore, open.

A mortuary papyrus, published by Denon,[23] belongs to *Osarkon,* a high-priest of Ammon-Ra; whose grandfather was a king *Miamun-Osarkon.* The genealogy is given thus:—

King *Miamun Osarkon*
|
High Priest *Šešonk* — *Nestautaχut*
|
Priest *Osarkon.*

The question may be, whether this Osarkon is the first or second of his name. His throne-shield is wanting; but, since the addition *si-bast* is also wanting to the name *Osarkon II.*, the nearest supposition is for *Osarkon I.* True it is, *Osarkon II.* had a son *Šešonk*, whom we have found twice mentioned as a prince, and who succeeded him as *Šešonk II.* But this prince has both times the same title, though not that of a high priest of Ammon Ra, like the *Šešonk* in Denon's papyrus.

On the contrary, we learn from another monument a High Priest *Šešonk*, son of a King *Miamun Osarkon*, who probably is the same as the *Šešonk*, High Priest, in question, son of King *Miamun Osarkon*. I refer to the statue of the Nile deity, *Hapi*, in the British Museum,[24] published by myself, and so much commented on by Leemans, Birch, Mariette, and others. On the side of its back pillar this High Priest *Šešonk* is represented, and in various inscriptions he takes the curiously remarkable title of a "Lord of the Upper and Lower Country," "Chief of the . . . Soldiers of Egypt," and "High Priest of Ammon Ra, King of the Gods." He has only one shield and bears the royal Uräus on his forehead,[25] but his name *Šešonk* has the addition, *Miamun*, preceding it, and is enclosed with it in a king's shield; and there follows after his shield the usual royal title, *ti anχ χa ra* (life-giving, like the sun). All this inclines to a very peculiar rank of this High Priest *Šešonk*, that was scarcely usurped, as he mentions his royal father, *Miamun Osarkon*, with the usual titles as regnant and existing king, and also his mother, who certainly did not bear the title as queen, but who was, nevertheless, the daughter of a King *Miamun Hor Petuχanu*. Their genealogy will be as follows:—

King *Miamun Hor Petuχanu*
|
Daughter *Rakamat* — King *Miamun Osarkon*
|
High Priest *Miamun Šešonk*.

Since we know the royal fathers of both Kings Osarkon, King *Hor Petuχanu* must stand outside this dynasty, as his name also points to the XXI. Dynasty. Whether he was contemporary with Osarkon, the circumstance that, behind his name, we have the addition *ti anχ*, is no certain proof. The relation of these two royal names, in my opinion, allow no other explanation than that we assume that Hor Petuχanu was the last king of the XXI. Dynasty, and who, possibly, during his lifetime, had to abdicate his throne to the Bubastian, *Šešonk*; whether from a defect of male heirs, or from some other unknown cause. The Osarkon of the Nile statue can be no other than *Osarkon I.* He took to wife Rakamat, daughter of the last Tanitic king, and possibly united thereby the last descendant of the seceding royal family with the new house founded by his father. That we have in this Osarkon the first of his name appears also from the circumstance that his name is neither joined to a king's shield nor does it bear the addition of the second Osarkon, *si-bast*; and, lastly, the identity of the priestly title of this Prince *Šešonk* with that of the Prince *Šešonk* in Denon's papyrus, whom we must not confuse, on account of this title, with the son of Osarkon II.

This just-cited monument giving us at the same time the name of a king of the XXII. and XXI. Dynasty, obliges us to cast at least a passing look at the XXI. Dynasty. We do not yet fully gain their names from the monuments, and the names we discover can be brought in only very imperfect coincidence with Manetho's Lists. Difficulties thence arise for the restoration of the Dynasty, into which we cannot now enter. I remark, therefore, only what follows to explain the shields noted in the tables.

That King *Siamun Herhor* was the first of his dynasty is undoubted, according to the Theban monuments previously mentioned. In *Xonsu* Temple we find after his wife, *Semet*, *Pianχ* mentioned as the eldest of his numerous sons. There can scarcely be a doubt that he is the same as the high priest *Pianχ*, whom we find repeatedly mentioned as father of the reigning high priest *Pisem*. This *Pianχ* never appears alone, or with the royal titles, like his father and his son; and, if he reigned, Pisem must have been called son of king, not son of the high priest, Pianχ. Nor, as the same, could *Pianχ*, the father of the royal high priest, have stood beyond the line of succession, otherwise the Dynasty would have broken through. We must, therefore, assume that *Pianχ*, the eldest son of Siamun Herhor, died before his father, that, according to the direct hereditary succession, the throne immediately descended to *Pisem*, the son of the high priest, *Pianχ*. He would, therefore, though third in descent, be the second of his dynasty. He assumed, in addition to the title of high priest, which he retained, the royal prænomen and title; without including his name in a shield on the existing monuments. But this was supplied by his son, *Menχeperra*, who calls himself, "Son of *Miamun Pisem*," and then encloses the name of his father in a shield.[26] He himself also assumed the royal shields, but writes in the first of the two, like his ancestor, Herhor, only "High Priest of Ammon;" in another place, in lieu thereof, we have the title, "King of Lower and Upper Egypt." This departure from the previous Pharaonic custom shows sufficiently the preponderating hieratical character of the first kings of this Dynasty.

Behind *Menχeperra* some kings seem wanting, that we do not yet know from the monuments. But the last kings of this Dynasty have renounced, at least in their titles, something of this priestly character.

The ruins of the old town, *Tanais*, from which the XXI. Dynasty sprung, are now unimportant. I found, during my visit thither, only the remnants of a moderately sized temple, adorned, however, with a great number of small granite obelisks; these lie around, dispersed, and all bear the shields of Ramses II., the Great, from whom, probably, the principal portion of the temple has its origin.[27]

On a broken royal statue, close to the left calf, stood the inscription of the monarch represented, of which, unfortunately, the throne-shield was alone preserved.[28] It seems that this king belonged to the Tanitic XXI. Dynasty, for which the style of the hieroglyphics speaks. The same is certainly the case with the name of King *Miamun Petuχanu*, which I find stamped on the tiles of the outer circuit of the temple, for which the throne name is wanting; if it be not accidentally that of the above statue, which will, for the present, connect with it, without vouching this as certain.

The connexion of King *Petuχanu* with the XXI. Dynasty appears from the inscription on a small strip of leather in the Turin Museum, from which we learn that he had as son a High Priest *Pisem*. We know that the successors to the throne were generally high priests of Ammon, and thus the second King Pisem, named on the monuments, is given as son and successor of King Petuχanu. This *Pisem II.* added also to the buildings of the *Xonsu* temple at Karnak, and appears there with both his royal shields.

We have now only King *Hor-Petuχanu* remaining, who, by the addition of *Hor* proves himself the second *Petuχanu*. He is the same from whom the throne descended to the XXII. Dynasty and to its founder, *Šešonk I.*, whose daughter, *Rakamat*, was married to *Osarkon I.*, son of *Šešonk I.*

With this new Dynasty new dynastic names appear, and this change is now greater than otherwise usual. In the family names of the XXII. Dynasty, the foreign character above noted, in contrariety to those of the earlier dynasties, is not to be denied. The names, *Šešonk*, *Osarkon*, *Takelut*, are plainly not originally Egyptian; and Birch,[29] who first drew attention to the circumstance, believes in these and the other royal names of that period, rather their ascription to Assyrian and Aramic forms. *Šešonk*, written in Scripture, *Šišaq*, he compares with *Šēšak*, which, in two passages of Jeremiah (xxv. 26; li. 41), is translated in the Septuagint *Babylon*. *Osorchon* he thinks he can identify with the Assyrian *Sargon*, from the restored cuneiform inscriptions—*Takelut* with the vernacular name of the Tigris, and that of the Chaldæan king, *Tiglat*,—and *Namrut* with the Hebrew *Nimrod*. He concludes from this similarity of names a political connexion betwixt Egypt and Assyria, which had already commenced under the XXI. Dynasty (pp. 168, 169, 170),[30] and upon intermarriages betwixt their two royal families; by which, alone, names like Nimrod (The Lord, in Assyrian) would have been introduced into Egypt. I can, however, not concur in this conclusion of my learned friend, though Mariette,[31] too, has taken the same view, and extended it.

The certainly un-Egyptian names of the Bubastic Dynasty appear to me to prove nothing more than that *Šešonk I.* had sprung from an Asiatic, probably Semitic family, settled at Bubastis. Nor is it thereby denied that Egyptian kings may not occasionally have given their daughters in marriage to foreign friendly rulers, as well as have received daughters from them. We know that Solomon had to wife the daughter of a Pharaoh,[32] and, according to Syncellus, Jeroboam also, during his flight into Egypt, married a daughter of *Šešonk.*[33] As early as Ramses II. we see a wife or princess, daughter of the *Xeta,* received as queen in Egypt. She is represented on a stele at Abu Simbel. Her hieroglyphical name is included in a royal ring, and composed after Egyptian form; and therefore substituted for her home-name. Behind it marches her father, known as a foreigner by his high pointed cap.[34] Another Asiatic royal daughter is mentioned in the interesting stele of the reign of Rameses XII., at Paris.[35] Her name, originally *Bent-reš,* was changed for an Egyptian royal shield, when she became the wife of the king.

But such unions afford no reason for transferring dynastic names from one nation to another. This happened only on conquest. The Ethiopians, Persians, Macedonians, Greeks, retained their names in Egypt, although they added all the other titles and additions in the Egyptian tongue.

Foreign names are easily distinguishable from Egyptian in hieroglyphical texts. The rule will rarely fail: that all names *written purely phonetically* are of foreign origin; whilst the true Egyptian names have, almost without exception, one or more ideographic characters. The reason is that their names, like those of all old nations, were significant; and hieroglyphical writing was so essentially ideographic that by far the majority of the substantive words have as a centre an ideographical character, round which, in various modes, the phonetic signs range themselves. It happens also that foreign names are at least partially cut up into significant Egyptian syllables, and then appear written seemingly ideographically, as when the name Arsinoë, with the figure *ari* at the beginning, is written : such, however, are rare and late exceptions. It oftener happens in early periods that foreign names are resolved in single-sounding Egyptian signs that are not generally found in the Egyptian alphabet, which can here only mean sound-signs, and which were easily cognisable as such from their position.

The rule for foreign royal names was that they were written with the common phonetic hieroglyphic, as Šabak, Tahraka, Darius, Xerxes, Alexander, Ptolemæus; and therefore, *e contrario,* from all names written in such manner it may be generally assumed that they are of foreign origin.

This is more especially the case with the names of the Bubastic Dynasty. No proof can be adduced that they were from Babylon, or any foreign royal race, whilst such supposition is decidedly contradicted by the names of the ancestors of *Šešonk I.* And indeed, we have earlier, amongst the private citizens of Bubastis, the names of two of the later members of this royal house, namely, *Namurot,* his father, and *Šešonk,* his grandfather. The royal names, therefore, had no reference to any relation with an Asiatic court, but merely to the family descent of the Bubasti.

It is necessary to suppose the population of the Delta, more especially of its eastern portion, which abutted on Palestine, as very mixed. The, for the most part, yet unexplained names of the children of Mizraim (Ludim, Anamim, Lehabim, Naphthuhim, Patrusim, Casluhim, with the Philistim, and Caphthorim), point to as many tribes living in the Delta (for the Patrusim alone can we look in Upper Egypt), or which have proceeded from it; and which scarcely all can belong to the race of Egyptians proper, but were reckoned to them in the sense of the oracle (Herod. II. 18) which called all those Egyptians who lived along the Nile, and drank its waters. The foreign settlers assumed, no doubt, for the greater part, the religion of the country; even the Israelites made no exception, and were, therefore, on the other hand, like Joseph and Moses, treated fully as Egyptians. The first became prime minister of the country, and married a daughter of the priest of Heliopolis; and, according to an Egyptian tradition, the latter was an Heliopolitan priest; though their origin was well-known, and not denied by themselves.

We need not therefore be surprised that a man of a foreign race, a native of Bubastis, raised himself to such a height in the state that he at last ascends the throne, and writes his name in the royal rings.

It is scarcely possible to reduce with certainty every single name to its Asiatic significance, but some comparison with Semitic names and races may be allowed. The primeval ancestor was called *Buiuoa,*[36] and with its first syllable we may compare the Semitic name בַּוַּי, *Bui* (Nehem. iii. 18). [The English version is *Bavai.*] For the three following names, *Maosen, Nebneša, Petut,* similar Semitic roots might be found. We have, then, *Šešonk,* which in Hebrew is well known, שִׁישַׁק *Šišeq* (*Šīšaq*); once also שׁוּשַׁק *Šušeq* (*Šūšaq*), in the Septuagint written Σούσακ and Σουσακίμ. Hieroglyphically, it is usually written *Šešonk,* and therefore Manetho has Σέσωγχις, since in Lower Egypt the *k* was easily changed into the Greek χ. If the name, as we assume, was Semitic, it was undoubtedly one and the same with *Šešeq* (*Šašaq*) of the Benjamites (1 Chron. viii. 14, 25), which is declared a contraction of שְׁקַשֵׁק desiderium [affection], (Gesen. Thesaur. p. 1478). It seems that it was intended to express the sharp guttural sound *q* in Egyptian, by the introduction of a nasal consonant before it. It is certainly remarkable that the orthography of the name oscillates, even in the hieroglyphics betwixt *Šešenk* and *Šešek*, in a manner which does not allow us to consider the omitted *n* as mere carelessness. The introduction of a foreign sound, not existing in the Egyptian language, explains this oscillation. But again, this name had, doubtless, nothing to do with the mystical spelling of Babylon, *Šešek* (שֵׁשַׁךְ *Šēšak*, Jer. xxv. xxvi. 51, 41).

The following name, *Namurot*, has been long since placed in conjunction with נִמְרֹד *Nemred, Nimrod* (from the root מָרַד), the son of *Kuš*, Greek Νεβρώδ.

After the irruption of the Egyptian king, *Šešonk*, into Palestine, we have in Chronicles (2, xiv. 9) another by the Kushite, *Zereχ* (*Zeraχ*). It is extremely ready here to think on the successor of *Šešonk*, King *Osarkon* (Manetho's 'Οσορχών). That the writer of Chronicles (he of Kings does not mention it) calls the king departing from Upper Egypt a Kushite, as well as Taharka, the later Ethiopian king of Thebes, can scarcely justify any searching for a contrary opinion.[37] It is impossible to fancy an independent Ethiopian war-march to Palestine, during the reign of the XXII. Dynasty in Egypt. This notice seems to be of later origin than that of *Šešonk*, and may therefore explain the greater variation of the orthography. But as far as regards the prefixed Egyptian vowel, we find, besides the patronymic *Zerχi* (זַרְחִי *Zarχi*), its other form, *Azerχi* (אֶזְרָחִי *Izraχi*), where the subjoined *n* was possibly a derivative form. But then, also, the name of the long subsequent Assyrian king, *Sergun* (סַרְגּוֹן *Sargun*, Isa. xx. 1) cannot then be brought here into account.

For the name *Takelut* Birch has already introduced *Teglet* (תִּגְלַת, *Tiglath*).

Also, for the name *Šuput*,[38] as well as for the feminine *Karoama* and *Karomama*, for *Tašpu* and perhaps *Tentespeh*, we need not look for Egyptian etymologies; but, with this exception, all the other feminine names may have an Egyptian origin, which is not surprising. Amongst the kings of the Dynasty the only one not of a foreign appearance is *Peχi*. And, truly, is, in Egyptian, the male or the female cat;[39] and upon the Apis stele, No. 1907, dating from 2d *Peχi*, we have the name of a subject, *Peχi*, really with the determinative of the cat preceding it. This, as is well known, was a sacred animal in Egypt, and was especially worshipped at Bubastis, to whose local deity it was consecrated. This may have caused the exception to the general custom of retaining Semitic names, though, otherwise, a gradual introduction of Semitic against Egyptian names ought not to surprise us.

If we now cast a look upon the remaining dynasties, in regard to their etymological character, we find in the old monarchy nothing un-Egyptian except the VI. Dynasty, which was Ethiopian, ἐξ 'Ελεφαντίνης.[40] In this the names of the kings, Ati, Pepi, perhaps also Teta, Keka, seem to be of Ethiopic origin. The names of the Hyksos kings, which are only known from lists, not from monuments, were also, doubtless, of Semitic origin. The Theban dynasties then succeed; their names are as purely Egyptian as might be predicted from Upper Egyptian families. So also the XXI. and XXIII. Dynasties, which took their rise from Tanis, have only Egyptian names, with the exception of the 'Οσορχών of the XXIII., which seems only a reminiscence of the kings of the XXII.

The names of the Ethiopic XXV. Dynasty, *Šabaka, Šabatoka, Taharka,* are, according to their orthography, not less Egyptian than those of the Persian XXVII. In none of the names of these two Dynasties is an ideographic character, or any accordance with known Egyptian words.

But just as little doubtfully do the names of the Sebennytic XXX. Dynasty sound Egyptian; whilst those of the Mendesian XXIX. may rather be called in question, particularly the name *Hakor.*

Again, it appears to me certain that the kings of the XXVI. Saitic Dynasty were not originally of Egyptian, but probably of Libyan origin. The name, *Psemetik,* Ψαμμίτιχος, Ψαμμήτιχος, invariably rendered purely phonetically, has a decided foreign appearance. The same is the case with the second dynastic name, *Nekau,* Νεχάω, Νεκώς; for that in his name the steer,  *ka,* appears occasionally, instead of the arms, ⊔ does not make the name more Egyptian. We can form no opinion on the names, Stephinates and Nechepso, as they do not appear on the monuments. Apries-Hophra is formed from the Egyptian throne-shield of Psametich I., a name, therefore, that does not come into consideration here; *Aahmas* ("Αμασις), on the contrary, the usurper, had an Egyptian name (the young moon), and was, perhaps, of Egyptian race; though he called his son *Psametik.*

Saïs lay on the western Nile-arm, towards the Libyan frontier, and was therefore as fully thronged with Libyan settlers as the towns on the Pelusian arm with Semitic ones. Possibly, Saïs, the town of Neith (Athene) was in nearer relation to the Libyans; for we hear[40*] that the Libyans worshipped the Athene as an *indigenous* deity, and that the virgins observed a martial feast in her honour. The symbols of Neith, the Libyan bow and arrow, may also indicate Libya. During the Persians' rule we hear of revolts of Egyptians and Libyans against Persians, and Herodotus mentions expressly the *Libyan Inaros* ('Ινάρώς ὁ Λίβυς, III., 12, 15), who rose against Darius. This Libyan Inaros was the son of a *Psammitichos,* as Herodotus also tells us (VII., 7) and may, therefore, have been a descendant of a Libyan family at Saïs. The names of both *Inaros* and his son, *Thannyris,* are not of Egyptian sound.

Is now our supposition correct, that the Saitic House of Psametich was, in its race, of Libyan descent? It is extremely easy to suppose the same for the XXIV.[41] and XXVIII. Dynasty, which also sprung from Saïs, and which may have been in nearer relation to one another than has been hitherto supposed.

This leads me to some remarks on the relations of the XXVI. Dynasty to those near it, which I make here, since, latterly, this period has often been discussed, and many newly discovered monuments give a welcome confirmation to opinions on these Dynasties, formed long ago.

Since 1840 I had gained the conviction, and adduced it in my "Chronology of the Egyptians" (I., pp. 313, 429), that Manetho, in his historical work, could not have introduced dynasties with a *single* king, as is the case in the XXIV. and XVIII. Dynasties. One dynast forms no dynasty, and a *single* usurper would have closed in to the foregoing Dynasty, as was the case with Amasis, though even he had his son as successor. To this we may add that the name of a regnant father is known to history for Bocchoris, who now alone forms the XXIV. Dynasty; and that for Amyrtæus, the single king of the XXVIII. Dynasty, according to the lists it is expressly recorded that the Persians acknowledged his son, Pausiris, as king. For these and other reasons, I assumed that these two Dynasties of the list were incomplete. The strongly expressed national feeling in Egypt for the oppressed legitimacy of their indigenous monarchs makes it much more probable that the three Semitic Dynasties, XXIV., XXVI., and XXVIII., were uninterruptedly connected; and that the imposed rule, from conquest, of the Ethiopian XXV. and of the Persian XXVII. Dynasty, were viewed by Manetho, according to his sense of legitimacy, only as *bye-kings* [*Neben Könige*]. This view gains important support from the consideration that the three first kings of Manetho's XXVI. Dynasty must have ruled contemporary with the Ethiopian. For this is proved by the perfectly trustworthy relation of Herodotus, and is indirectly confirmed by the entire want of monuments of those oppressed kings previous to Psametich I.[41*]

Amongst the monuments from the Apis caves, brought to Paris by Mariette, whose examination was permitted me last year, a stele (No. 2037) has been brought to light, which perfectly confirms this relative position of the first Psametich to the Ethiopic Dynasty, and permits it to be further carried out. M. de Rougé, whose notice the importance of this stele for our purpose has not escaped, has already considered it in his latest essay,[42] instructive as always, and has treated more particularly its chronological bearing.

This stele is dated from the twenty-first year of Psametich I., and speaks of an Apis which died in the twentieth year of the same king, and had made its entry into Memphis in the twenty-sixth of Taharka. Therefrom, it is immediately evident that Taharka, if he died in the same year, and the Apis had lived its full complement of 25 years since its birth or consecration, that it could have died, at the utmost, but six years before Psametich's accession. M. de Rougé gives to the steer 24 years' life, to Taharka, as Bunsen does, a government of 28 years, and includes betwixt his last year and the first of Psametich two years of anarchy. The number of regnant years of Psametich and his successors, to Cambyses, he fixes (p. 139) as I do,[43] but moves the years B.C. altogether two years higher back; because he places the conquest of Cambyses B.C. 527, instead of 525.

I have before given my reasons[44] why it appears entirely arbitrary to depart from the general opinion, based upon express ancient testimony, that this conquest took place in 525. All the objections to it are groundless, and the doubt I myself raised formerly against 525 depended entirely upon a monumental and official date, vouched to me from another quarter, namely, of a *fourth* year of Cambyses, which truly *forced* a departure from these written testimonials, but which was found subsequently erroneous, as I mentioned in the August monthly report, 1854, to the Academy. Whether my learned colleague, M. de Rougé, has taken into consideration the reasons that I advanced against the year 525, and not found them satisfactory, does not appear from his last essay, in which he only remarks (p. 39, note): "La stèle funéraire de l'Apis mort l'an IV. de Darius montre clairement qu'on a eu raison de compter ainsi" (namely, 525).[45] This same stele (No. 2284) offered, certainly, great difficulty, as I have already mentioned,[46] since might be read upon it that an Apis, born in the fifth year of Cambyses, died in the fourth year of Darius, eight years and some months old. Cambyses had, therefore, lived one year longer than the canon allowed. This difficulty might possibly have been removed by allowing Herodotus to have been in error. But, on my examination of the stele, it appeared that the longevity of the steer was given there as of *seven*, not of *eight* years, of which Messrs. de Rougé and Mariette convinced themselves, upon a closer examination.

The inscription is much damaged, but still its calculation may be substantially made good when we supply what is wanting, as follows:—

An Apis [born]	in V. year, V. month, [XXVIII.] days [of Cambyses]
He is brought into Phtha's temple .	? ?
He dies	in IV. yr., IX. m., [III. d. of Darius]
He is buried	in IV. yr., XI. m., XIII. of Darius
He is old	7 years, 3 months, 5 days.

The date of the stele is that of the death, and is perfectly preserved. Proceeding from this date, IV. years, XI. months, XIII. days of Darius, 70 days back, we gain the date of the death, IV. years, IX. months, III. days of the same king. This date we find in the eighth stele, but so that the number III. of the days is broken off; but which we can supply from the date of burial. This restoration is confirmed by the stelæ, 2286 and 2290, on which the day of death is plainly preserved.[47] The life of the steer is fully noted again in the last line. If we count backwards from the death-date 7 years, 3 months, and 5 days, we reach the fourth last year of Cambyses, VI. months, III. days, as the birth-day. This does *not* agree with the numbers of the ninth line, in which we can alone search for the birth-day, although the group which designates the birth is destroyed at the end of line 8. Here we have a V. year, namely of Cambyses, whose shield is also destroyed, for the V. month is preserved, beyond doubt, and of the number of days so much that it may be seen that it is a large one, at least above twenty. I suppose, therefore, that the V. month and XXVIII. days were put down, and, therefore, that either in reckoning the duration of life from the day of birth, or of the day of birth from the duration of life, a mistake of five days was made, by not taking the five epagomenæ of the first year into account.[48]

Dr. Hincks, in an essay, *On the Chronology of the XXVI. Egyptian Dynasty* (*Trans. of the R. Ir. Ac.*, vol. XXII., 1855, p. 423, *seqq.*) agrees for the length of the separate reigns of the XXVI. Dynasty with me and M. de Rougé; but he pushes the conquest of Egypt by Cambyses, which he placed, it seems, before any one else, in 1841,[49] at B.C. 527, now a year further back, to 528; so that, at once, all the commencements of the reigns of the XXVI. Dynasty fall *three* years earlier than usual. He supports himself upon the emendation of a passage of Africanus, already proposed in 1841. This reads, at present: Καμβύσης, ἔτη ε′ τῆς ἑαυτοῦ βασιλείας Περσῶν ἐβασίλευσεν Αἰγύπτου ἔτη ϛ′; it was, however, amended by Scaliger, and concurred in by Boeckh, Bunsen, C. Müller, Fruin, &c., so far that instead of the first ἔτη they wrote ἔτει. Hincks, however, would retain the ἔτη, but change the number ε′ into θ′, and translates, therefore: "Cambyses reigned nine years over his own kingdom of the Persians, and six over Egypt," so that Cambyses had conquered Egypt in the fourth year of his Persian empire. He is strengthened in this opinion by believing he has found on the Egyptian monuments a ninth year of Cambyses, and endeavours to explain this divergence from Ptolemy's Canon—that he gives Cambyses only eight regnal years in Persia—that Ptolemy reckoned according to Babylonian custom, according to which, the year in which a monarch died was counted to him, and not to his successor. This Babylonian usage may be difficult to establish, and, even if existing, we still know that in Ptolemy's Canon the regal numbers were counted as customary in Egypt, as has been proved by Ideler, Boeckh, &c. There could, therefore, have been no exception for the Persian kings. The variation, mentioned in his note (p. 426), in the count of the canon from the count on the monuments gives here no elucidation. But when it is therein asserted that in the Leyden papyrus,[50] which I vindicated to Ptolemy Philadelphus, there is a different count to that of the canon, because the papyrus reckons from Philadelphus's accession to the government, but the canon from the death of Soter two (not three) years later, this assertion is founded on an error, since the canon which gives Soter twenty years from A.N. 444 = B.C. 305, counts also from the entry of Philadelphus into the government, and not to the death of Soter; and ascribes, therefore, to Philadelphus, not 36 but 38 regnal years, viz., to A.N. 501 = B.C. 248-49. The agreement on this point betwixt the canon and Porphyry, as shown by Clinton and Ideler (Chronol. I., 357), &c., appears not capable of impeachment. The proposed emendation ἔτη ϑ′ instead of ἔτει ε′ may have, also, little to recommend it. The metathesis of the two vowels η and ει in MSS. belongs, as is well known, to those most common. The reading, ἔτει ε′, is, besides, protected by the corresponding passage in Eusebius,[51] which runs: Καμβύσης, ἔτει πέμπτῳ τῆς αὐτοῦ βασιλείας ἐβασίλευσεν ἔτη γ′, "Cambyses, anno regni sui XV. (*read* V.), regnavit in Ægyptios annis III." And, finally, the words themselves are opposed to the attempted construing; for, τῆς ἑαυτοῦ βασιλείας Περσῶν ἐβασίλευσεν, "he reigned over his own kingdom of the Persians," would, to say the least, be an uncommon expression; and we should rather connect, ἔτη ϑ′ τῆς ἑαυτοῦ βασλείας, nine years of his government, Περσῶν ἐβασίλευσεν, he ruled over the Persians: but then, at all events, we must follow with Αἰγύπτου δὲ, or τῆς δὲ Αἰγύπτου. It would, then, however, have been here to no purpose that the author, who merely enumerates the Egyptian reigns shortly one after another, should suddenly give the period of Persian rule for a king, and put his Egyptian at the side, when the Eusebian form is the only natural one—"in the time of five years of his Persian rule he reigned (four) years over Egypt." The fifth year is given both by Africanus and Eusebius, and from them, Syncellus, also, has taken it (p. 211, *A.* 209, *B.* 236, B.C.) into his computation: Πέρσαι ἐκράτησαν ἀπὸ ε′ ἔτους Καμβύσου. No Egyptian chronologer had any cause to alter it, whilst a change in the number of years that Cambyses reigned in Egypt is easily explained from the confusion into which the entire chronology of this period had fallen. What, finally, is supposed to confirm the emendation, ἔτη θ′, which the monuments are supposed to offer, that stele only seems here meant, on which was read that the Apis which died in the fourth year of Darius was more than eight years old.[52] This same stele teaches us with new evidence that Cambyses, as the canon rightly notes, ruled only *eight* years in Persia. It also appears, with great probability, that the steer, wounded in the thigh by Cambyses, did not, as the legend added, die from the injury, nor was secretly buried, but that it was no other than the animal mentioned in this stele which was born in the year of the conquest, and did not die till the fourth of Darius.

There is, however, another circumstance to be mentioned, which still remains obscure. Amongst the Apis-stelæ in the Louvre, there is one which dates from Year VI., Month XI. of *Cambyses*; since, as proved in the learned treatise of M. de Rougé, "Sur la Statuette Naophore du Vatican," the throne-shield belongs to Cambyses. On this shield the steer is represented, and the king kneels before him in adoration, cognisable only by throne-shield and standard. In the third line from the bottom a seventeenth year is mentioned, and behind the date in the first line a group is found which refers to the burial of an Apis. Unfortunately, I possess the date of this stele only in a copy, and cannot, therefore, judge whether from the remaining context of the inscription any further particulars on the cause of this Proskynema may be observed. How it would have been possible that an Apis which lived seven years could have been born in the fifth year, and that in the sixth another was buried, is, so far as hitherto the facts are known, not apparent.

But since, as far as I see, nothing can be drawn herefrom to give any weight to the year 527 as that of the conquest, I return from this digression to the point that further doubts as to that acceptation should be supported by new and valid reasons, which do not appear to me to have been hitherto advanced. While, therefore, for us the first year of Psametich I. falls on B.C. $\frac{663}{662}$ = Nabon. 85, De Rougé places it at $\frac{665}{664}$ = Nabon. 83. He takes for the last year of Taharka, $\frac{668}{667}$, and for the first, $\frac{695}{694}$.

The three reigns which Manetho lets precede Psametich he considers as contemporaneous, and unimportant for chronology. "La chronologie devait les retrancher complètement de ses calculs" (p. 38). If, however, under the rule of the Ethiopian kings a new indigenous dynasty could commence under *Stephinates*, whilst Taharka was still recognised throughout the land as king *de facto*, and as such was recognised even under Psametich, it is evident that the right of Stephinates could not be founded upon a violent usurpation, but must have rested upon legitimate grounds: that is, the XXIV. Dynasty of Tnephacthus and Bocchoris must have been continued in direct lineal succession to B.C. $\frac{684}{685}$, the first of Stephinates, notwithstanding the Ethiopian conquest. A trace of a genuine tradition for a great number of kings for the XXII. Dynasty may, possibly, be recognised in the use of *Bocchoridæ* made by Eusebius in the *Series Regum* of this dynasty, instead of the single name, Bocchoris.

With the death of the last of the Bocchoridæ the legitimate succession must have passed to that line of the Saitic House nearest related; for the XXVI. Dynasty is expressly called *Saitic*. But there seem to have been numerous pretenders to the crown, and one of the Ethiopian claimants even to have been acknowledged, though dependent. For, besides the direct ancestors of Psametich which Manetho names, we find upon the monuments other kings, who reigned contemporary with the ancestry of Psametich, and who dared to use royal rings in their inscriptions. The names of these kings are given in the lithographic table (Pl. II.) herewith; from which will be perceived how the family of this side branch was also united to the family of Psametich by marriage. It appears that this Saitic branch, on the interruption of the elder branch under the Ethiopic rule, was not, possibly, the next legitimate, but that one most favoured by those in power; since we do not find on the monuments the ancestors of Psametich, but Kings *Kašen* and *Panχi* mentioned as such. It is, therefore, in conformity, when we find it noted that the Ethiopians murdered the father of Psametich, and drove him away into Syria; and that we at the same time find two kings called *Panχi*, perhaps the descendants of Psametich's father-in-law, with the same name, amongst the persecutors of Taharka, in his Ethiopian residence at the hill Barkal. A similar conflict of various lines was one of the principal causes of the formation of the well-known Dodecarchy, and we shall scarcely go wrong if, besides Psametich, we also take King *Panχi* and the Phtha-priest, Herodotus's *Sethos*, for participators in the Dodecarchian hierarchy, who again raised jealousies and expelled Psametich, doubtless on account of his legitimacy, till they at last were obliged to submit to his single supremacy. When, therefore, Amasis, who was a native, not of Sais, but of the Saitic Nome, had dethroned Apries, his legitimate king, we find him having raised a lady of the former pretender-family of *Panχi* to the throne—a matter that would scarcely have happened without farther political views.

I also call attention to the separate family branch of the *Pallades* of Ammon, which on our Table (Pl. II.) represents the connexion of the two Saitic lines. These were probably all (for hitherto but one has not been proven so) daughters, half-sisters, and subsidiary wives, who, beyond their priestly office, must have held a very honoured relative position to the king's, even more respected than that of the real queens, a title they never receive. The first title "Holy Lady of Ammon," was borne even by the ancestral mother of the new kingdom, *Aahmas Nofretari*;[53] her second, or, as more fully written, signified another high hierarchical rank, and is met singly not earlier than the end of the XX. Dynasty. Strabo, xvii., p. 816, says of them: *τῷ Διί, ὃν μάλιστα τιμῶσιν, εὐειδεστάτη καὶ γένους λαμπροτάτου παρθένος ἱερᾶται, ἃς καλοῦσιν οἱ Ἕλληνες παλλάδας.* This reading is found in all MSS., as well as in the Epitome, and in Eustatius (Odyss. xiii., 300; Il., i. 200), and is therefore preferable to the expression used by Diodorus (i., 47), *παλλακίδες Διός*, because Strabo immediately mentioning *παλλακεύειν*, says: *αὕτη δὲ καὶ παλλακεύει καὶ σύνεστιν, οἷς βούλεται, μέχρις ἂν ἡ φυσικὴ γένηται κάθαρσις τοῦ σώματος· μετὰ δὲ τὴν κάθαρσιν δίδοται πρὸς ἄνδρα· πρὶν δὲ δοθῆναι, πένθος αὐτῆς ἄγεται μετὰ τὸν τῆς παλλακείας καιρόν.* Diodorus mentions the graves of these wives of Ammon in a separate Theban rock-cleft, which we can still point out. They contain the inscriptions of royal wives and daughters, which seem all to have belonged to the XIX. and XX. Dynasties. Some of them bear the title, "holy lady," that is, of Ammon, and that, too, besides [hieroglyphs] "royal wife," so that it was not then exclusive. As we find the first designation confined to princesses, it seems evident that Strabo's added notice does not refer to the earlier periods: but, if not altogether a capricious extension of the circumstance that these Ammon-priestesses were also subordinate wives of the kings, we must receive it as a later abatement of the custom; perhaps since the Persian epoch, beyond which I have not found these titles, or possibly also later. It was then desirable to change the old designation, παλλάδες, which originally signified only virgin-priestesses devoted to the god, into παλλακίδες.

In the genealogy of the XXVI. Dynasty, here given, King *Kašen* or *Kašet* appears as *father* of Ameniritis,[54] for so, indeed, he is named on all the monuments on which I have found him;[55] it must, therefore, be an error, when De Rougé makes him a *son* of Ameniritis. But my learned colleague has certainly hit the truth when he supplies the fragmentary family-name on a very beautifully cut Parisian stele (Prisse, Mon., pl. IV.), on which only the closing figures, [hieroglyphs] can be made out, by *Panχi* [cartouche]. The statue found by Greene at Medînet Habu would have instructed him that Panχi was the husband of Ameniritis, and therefore that Mutiritis, the daughter of Panχi, was a sister of *Šepuntepu*,[56] because the last, as already shown, was a daughter of Ameniritis. To the name Mutiritis another genealogy is coupled, which leads to *Tentχeta*, the wife of Amasis.

I have formerly connected this Ameniritis with Eusebius's King Ammeres (Armen),[57] whom he adduces with the epithet Æthiops, as the first king of the XXVI. Dynasty. Similarity in the name, the high rank of the lady, and the uncertainty of her origin, might have been the easy inducement. But now, as it appears to me, this supposition must be given up. For, besides that Ammeris appears in the Lists expressly as a male, if we take the reign of Taharka as at least 26 years, there would scarcely be found room for an intervening rule of this Ameniritis. The special honour shown her in the inscriptions, and namely by the *double shields*, we find repeated for the other wives of Ammon. But what most contradicts our previous assumption is, that she stood in no relation to the Ethiopian kings, and was clearly not of Ethiopic origin. She was the daughter of a king contemporary with, and therefore subordinate to, the Ethiopians, and the wife of a king who had a known Egyptian name; she belonged to a race of Theban priestesses that we find in earlier dynasties, and which would scarcely connect itself with the foreign conquerors as intimately as with the native kings, and which is therefore not recognisable amongst the Ethiopic dynasties: her own, and the name of her two daughters are thoroughly Egyptian. All this is opposed to the idea that, under the name of Ammeris Æthiops, she should be designated as regent of the country; of itself very exceptionable.

The answer is ready to the inquiry, how Eusebius came to the name of Ammeris. I doubt not that he took it, like much else, from the false Sothis, who intercalates betwixt Ταράκης and Στεφινάθης a king whom he calls 'Αμαής; which is plainly only a variation of Ammeres. This Sothis, it is well known, closed the series of Egyptian kings by "Αμωσις (Amasis),[58] and introduced, therefore, his Amaes, to complete the ninth number of the XXVI. Dynasty. Eusebius, to whom this Sothis was a weighty authority, omitted Psamenitos at the end, and introduced, therefore, also his Ammeres, but added the epithet Αἰθίοψ; probably on his own authority, since he found, in Africanus, Stephinates, as head of the Saitic Dynasty.

The Holy Lady, *Šepuntepu,* is known as the wife of Psametich I.,[59] and mother of the Holy Lady, *Nitakret Mimut.* M. de Rougé considers this Nitocris as the same Holy Lady Nitocris who appears on the sarcophagus in the British Museum, *Anχnes Ranofrehet,* as wife of Psametich II.; who would then have married his aunt, which is not very probable. The distinction of these two Nitocris appears, however, more evident, from the circumstance that the daughter of Psametich I. has the bye-name, *Mimut;* but the wife of his grandson has, on the sarcophagus, the second name, *Šeretpimuntu.*[60] We may, therefore, conclude from the genealogical relations that *Nitakret Mimut* was the wife of her half-brother, *Nekau II.*, and the mother of *Nitakret-Šeretpimentu.* This last we know as mother of *Anχes Ranofrehet,* who probably united herself to *Uaphris,* of whom we know no other wife.

We know only three queens of this Dynasty. Of them the first, has been met hitherto only on the fragment of a column in Medînet Habu. The title is, indeed, lost, but it may be supplied with the greatest probability, from the group, usually connected with it. Of the other names contained on this fragment, Ameniritis, Sepuntepu, Psametich I., and Nitocris (Mimut), the last alone is mentioned as living. The queen, therefore, quoted as dead, could only be the wife of Psametich I. The second queen is *Taχot,* who appears on the sarcophagus of *Anχnes* as mother of *Psametich II.;* consequently as wife of *Nechao II.* The places in which mention is made of this queen might give cause for doubts, and are construed by Birch[61] and De Rougé as if *Taχot* was the daughter of *Anχnes;* and probably therefore, supported thereby, the latter makes her the wife of *Psametich III.*[62] But by further examination the above passages are capable of *only one* explanation. One place reads so: that is (omitting the immaterial groups), the Holy Lady, *Anχnes Ranofrehet,*[63] the royal daughter of King *Psametik;* her mother, the holy "Tet," ***Nitakret;*** (*iri-s*) the queen ***Taχot.*** De Rougé[64] translates the group by "her (*Anχnes'*) daughter," as before, "her (*Anχnes'*) mother." But this is contrary to usage. In a filiation, such as is here adduced for the better designation of a defunct party, after father and mother, the daughter is never introduced; as otherwise was not to be expected. Besides, *iri,* or *irit,* in general is *never used substantively* for "son" or "daughter," instead of or or and their feminines, but merely *verbally* for "begotten," or "born," both from father or mother; could as well mean "she bore," but not "her daughter;" besides that, in the latter case, *irites,* must have been written. As the characters, which are here very legible, stand, they give no sense. Luckily, the error attributable here to the mason or the copyist, is avoided in the second place. This reads: [65] We have here the same conjunction of the four names, only that instead of there stands *iri en,* "born of."[66] The name belonging to would, in the first, have to be sought for in the shield immediately preceding, as is done by Leemans; and then *Nitakret* would be born of *Taχot.* Such a construction could not be directly disproven, since we only hold as a supposition ***Nitakret Mimut,*** for the mother of ***Nitakret Šeretpimuntu.*** The circumstance that in both passages only not is written, militates against it. We must, therefore, refer the masculine to King Psametich, who was begotten of Queen Taχot. Doubtless, the passing over here the name of the mother must cause astonishment. This was, however, unavoidable in ascending genealogies in which father and mother are mentioned, and the line is continued only through the fathers, and which is so found in the genealogy of *Horpeson,* given above, in which, through all the generations, or refers to the last-named male; passing over all the preceding females. With the designation of gender any misapprehension is avoided. The words, "her mother (was) ***Nitakret,***" are to be understood as parenthetical.

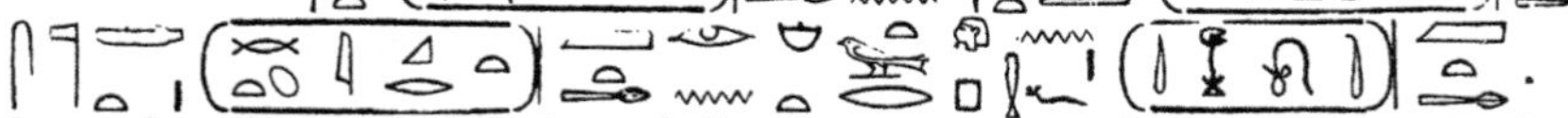

With, as appears to me, this alone defensible explanation, it is in accordance, that the Pallades, who play such a prominent part in this Dynasty as hierarchical women, form a continuous race, and that no Pallas can be found descended from a queen, nor any king from a Pallas.

From this same relationship of the Pallades, it follows that we are not to think of an identification of this Nitocris with the Doricha or Rhodopis of Grecian tales, which I have already confuted.[67] She was a Grecian courtesan, from Naukratis, who was perhaps raised by Psametich to the dignity of *queen,* but could not be received amongst the race of the Pallades.

I have, as a conjecture, joined the Pallas, *Anχnes-Ranofrehet,* to Uaphris, of whose wives neither monuments nor writers make mention. In its favour is the contemporaneousness of Uaphris and of Anχnes-Ranofrehet. Wilkinson and De Rougé give her to Amasis; Hincks[68] both to Uaphris and Amasis; and Birch[69] to a Psametich IV. and Amasis. She certainly is met on the monuments with Amasis, but not as queen; and if, as Pallas, she was his subordinate wife, that does not appear on the monuments. Their simultaneous connexion proves here as little as that of this same *Anχnes-Ranofrehet* with Psametich III.; it only affords another proof of the important position of the Pallades as joint regents of the country, which was not changed, even on the rise of a usurper like Amasis, much to his advantage. That Hincks holds King Psametich III. for a son of this *Anχnes-Ranofrehet* is directly contradicted by the Apis-stele, 2252, on which Prince Psametich is called son of King Amasis and Queen *Tentχeta.*

As regards the name of *Anχnes-Ranofrehet,* Rosellini, from a wrong placing of the *s* (Vol. VIII., p. 188), read *Sonchise* (*-Ranofrehet*). Birch[70] reads *Anch-sen-Pira-nefer-hat.* M. de Rougé[71] brings into comparison the name of the

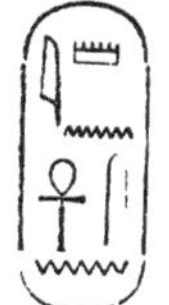

wife of King *Tutanχamun,* in the XVIII. Dynasty. This reads, *Anχe-senamun,* which De Rougé translates "*sa vie (vient) d'Amon,*" or "*elle vit de par Amon.*" From this he reads our name, "*Anchs-en-ra-nowre-het,*" and translates "*sa vie (vient) de Ra nofré het (Psametichus).*" Against his reading *Aχesenamun* it might be first objected that the group [hieroglyphs] might be put for [hieroglyphs] because the latter, especially in vertical order, as in the shield above, invited a transposition of the two last characters, on symmetrical grounds. We have, however, amongst the daughters of Amenophis IV. a name composed of the same group, and written sometimes [hieroglyphs], sometimes [hieroglyphs]:[71*] the last form, which is twice repeated, puts beyond a doubt the reading, *Anχesenpaten,* and consequently the queen, *Anχesenamun,* who reigned soon after her. But we have another case. If the order of the group [hieroglyphs] can only sound *anχesen,* equally certainly the group [hieroglyphs] must be read *anχnes,* because there was no reason to deviate from the natural symmetrical order, [hieroglyphs] in favour of the unsymmetrical [hieroglyphs] if *s* was here to be pronounced before *n*. This name is found at Karnak on a stele of Mr. Harris,[72] and on the sarcophagus of this princess, very frequently; and, as far as I know, is never arranged differently than in the quoted manner, which may have its cause in the pronunciation.[73] It is remarked by M. de Rougé that the first part of the name stands in necessary connexion with the second, and that a name, *Onkh nas* (*Anχnes*), without addition, would give the impossible sense, *elle a vécu*. But frequently we cannot translate the seemingly simplest phrases with perfect certainty. First, the name, *Anχnes*, seems really to be found without addition on a Leyden stele;[74] at least, the form of the female name, [hieroglyphs] cannot be otherwise taken than that the intermediate [hieroglyph] belongs to the end,—*Anχnes-t*. I call attention here, also, to the *nef*, masculine; *nes*, feminine, answering to the Greek participle in [hieroglyphs] *tutnef*, nominatus, [hieroglyphs] *tutnes*, nominata; properly, (qui) nominatus est; in the names of the Ptolemies, Ptolemæus *nominatus* (est) Alexander, Cleopatra *nominata* (est) Tryphæna. The feminine ending, *sen*, is found also without addition, as in the name [hieroglyphs] of a queen of the XIII. Dynasty,[75] besides the princely name, [hieroglyphs] of the same dynasty;[76] so that we might be inclined to divide these older names, with Birch, not, *Anχes-en-patenra*, *Anχes-en-amun*, but, *Anχ-sen-patenra*, *Anχ-sen-amun*. I do not venture to translate any of these names.

The queen, *Tentχeta*, was, according to the Apis-stele already mentioned, the daughter of the Phtha-priest, *Petnit*. We find the same name again as father of a *Šešonk*, who occupied so high a rank under the Anχnes-Ranofrehet, that in the Karnak[77] sculptures he is customarily placed behind her. His father already occupied the same post, as his titles prove; and it is, therefore, most improbable that the *Tentχeta*, raised by Amasis to be his queen, was a sister of *Šešonk*, and daughter of the same *Petnit* whom we meet in Karnak; though, from the conciseness of the legends, it is not expressed that he was also priest of Phtha.

In the valley, El Asasif, at Western Thebes, amongst the other private sepulchres of this Dynasty is also that of "The Great One of Pallas," ([hieroglyphs]) *Petnit*,[78] and here his parents, a *Psametik*, whose wife is *Tantbast*, are named. In an adjoining tomb we find another *Psametik*, who receives the title [hieroglyphs] as son of an *Uahprahet*, who held the same rank as [hieroglyphs] and is also called [hieroglyphs] and, was, therefore, the grandson of a king. As the father of this Uahprahet is called [hieroglyphs] *Petamun* (or *Petamunna ?*), and his mother [hieroglyphs] *Mutiritis*, one of them must have been the child of a king; though this is not here affixed to their inscriptions. But, as we already know and have produced a Princess *Mutiritis* as daughter of King Menχeperra Panχi, the supposition is certainly warranted, that the royal grandson, Uaphris, and his posterity to *Šešonk*, and the Queen Tentχeta, sprung from King Panχi.

Our genealogical table gives a synoptic view, how the family of the XXIV. Dynasty, which, supposing it extinct in the male line with King Panχi, united itself by two daughters of this king, in a two-fold manner, with the Saitic younger branch of the XXVI. Dynasty; inasmuch as, on the one hand, the Pallas, *Šepuntepu*, daughter of Panχi by the Pallas, Amuniritis, became the wife of Psametich I., and on the other, the princess, *Mutiritis*, also a daughter of Panχi, was the ancestress of the four links, Uahprahet, Psametik, Petnit, and *Šesonk*, who all held high offices in the service of the race of Pallades; the last of whom had a sister, raised by Amasis to the dignity of his queen, doubtless from regard to her royal descent.

The Ethiopic kings of the XXV. Dynasty march, without any apparent connexion with the native royal houses, alongside those of the XXIV. and XXVI. Dynasties; and were, doubtless, treated by Manetho as a collateral dynasty, and without any chronological union with the legitimate Pharaohs. The third and last king of the Ethiopic dynasty, the pious Taharka, retired voluntarily into Ethiopia, as it seems, because he could not any longer keep his standing against the growing power of the pretenders of the legitimate family; and left the much contested sovereignty of Egypt to the most powerful of the people, who, until the absolutism of Psametich, divided the government amongst twelve. He founded in his new residence at Meroë, at the holy hill, the present Barkal, a new, and the first native Ethiopic dynasty. His edifices there, the oldest Ethiopian of the entire south country, prove that he continued to govern there a series of years, and also entirely according to his accustomed Egyptian usages, whose civilization he transplanted into the abode of his fathers; and whose recognition we are able to trace in the twice recurrent name of *Panχi*, in the royal names of his immediate successors.

At p. 28 I have supposed an error in the computation of the epagomenæ on an Apis-stele. This induces me to make the following remarks on the numerals of the Apis-stelæ. The error of not taking into account, in an annual computation, the five epagomenæ, has been frequently made, and was first shown by Boeckh (Manetho, p. 347) for a Florentine stele of a Psametich. It recurs again on the Apis stele, No. 2243, whose Bull is said to have lived under Nechao 16 years, 7 months, and 17 days, whilst the computation makes it five days longer. M. de Rougé (*Not. sur quelques Textes Hiérogl., Tableau de Concorde,* Note 1) mentions this instance, but does not account the computation as an error, but intentional; and looks upon it as "la manière sacrée de compter les jours," without giving his reasons for this opinion: but, as all the other years betwixt birth and death are counted for full 365 days, a mode of reckoning could scarcely have been admitted by which the five epagomenæ of the first year (in the note we have "de la dernière [?] année") could have been skipped, and the true age be represented too short. M. de Rougé himself notices (Note 3) a Leyden stele on which the epagomenæ are brought in account. Also upon Mr. Harris's Stele (Sharpe, Eg. Inscr. I., 73; Prisse, Mon. pl. XXVI.) the epagomenæ are reckoned in, though Dr. Hincks (On an Eg. Stele, p. 5) is of a contrary opinion; since from XI. months, XV. days, to I. month, XX. days, are, with the epagomenæ, 70 days, as is required. is here namely the XV. day, and (which Hincks perhaps took for , 30) must here denote 20, as immediately after , 30. The same true computation of the epagomenæ recurs again on an Apis stele of the LII. year of Euergetes II., and is on more than one account remarkable; I therefore give its contents.

"In the year LII., month I. (read II., i.e. Phaophi), day XXVIII., "under the reign of King Ptolemy (IX.) and his sister, the Queen Cleo- "patra (II.), and of his queen, Cleopatra (III.), the three beneficent deities "( ) son and daughter[79] ( ) of King Ptolemy (V.) and of "Cleopatra (I.), the deities Epiphanes; on this day was this Apis-Osiris "deposited in this tomb (*ap pen*) in a sarcophagus of black stone, "after having undergone the holy usages for 70 days (during the mummifica- "tion).[80] His Majesty was born in the temple at Memphis in XXVIII. year, "V. month (Tobi), XXIV. days of King Ptolemy (IX.), and of his sister, "Queen Cleopatra (II.): he remained (, *χop-ref*, Copt. ϢΟΠ, manere) "in the temple at Memphis, from the year XXVIII. to the year XXXI., "month I. (Thoth) of the reign of King Ptolemy, and of his sister, Cleopatra, "and of his wife, Cleopatra. In the year XXXI., month I. (Thoth), day XX., "he went to Nilopolis, remained in the temple of the Nile the XXI. Thot, and "was received into the temple of Ptah (at Memphis) on XXIII. (Thoth) (under "the reign) of King Ptolemy, and of his sister, Cleopatra, and of his wife, "Cleopatra. He was on his throne[81] in the palace of Memphis ( )[82] 20 years, "11 months, and 22 days. This god ascended to heaven ( ) in the year LI., "month XII. (Mesore), day XXII., under the reign of King Ptolemy, and of "his sister, Cleopatra, and of his wife, Cleopatra: the fortunate life-time of this "god continued 23 years, 6 months, 29 days. This did (placing the stele) the "king, Ptolemy, and his sister, Cleopatra, and his wife, Cleopatra."

The synopsis of these dates is as follows :—

This Apis was born at Memphis .	in XXVIII. year,	V. month,	XXIV. da.
He remains there to	„ XXXI. „	I. „	(XIX.) „
He goes to Nilopolis	„ XXXI. „	I. „	XX. „
Remains there in the Nile temple .	„ — „	I. „	XXI. „
Returns to Memphis, and enthroned	„ — „	— „	XXIII. „
He dies	„ LI. „	XII. „	XXII. „
Is buried	„ LII. „	(II.) „	XXVII. „
He throned	20 years,	11 months,	[22 days.]
He lived	23 „	6 „	29 „

We find here much at variance with the historical accounts. When Ælian tells us that the newly discovered calf was brought up four months at the place of its birth, he seems to have understood this as a minimum ; for we find that this Apis, which was born in the very temple of Memphis, passed more than two years and seven months there before its consecration. The day to which he was kept there is, most probably from mistake, omitted. I have supplied the XIX. day, because on the following he is taken to Nilopolis, and his stay, so far, continued exactly two years and eight months. The same figure would be brought out if we allow two days for the journey to Nilopolis, and write XVIII. instead of XIX., and then include the last day ; as frequently, but erroneously, occurs in Egyptian calculations. Diodorus tells us the Bull remained at Nilopolis[83] 40 days. Our animal remained only *one*, or, if the following day was not spent on the return, only *two* days in the temple of the Nile, namely, the XXI. and XXII. Thoth ; for, on the XXIII. he was already returned to the temple of Phtha, and enthroned there. As he dies on XXII. Mesore of the LII. year, he must have lived 23 years, 6 months, and 28 days ; the inscription says 29, as both the first and last day was included. After his return to Memphis, however, he had passed on his throne, 20 years, 11 months, and 22 days ; since, evidently by a mistake of the writer or sculptor, the 22 days of the date in the following line are misplaced here.[84] From the day of death to that of burial 70 days elapsed, as is here and frequently expressly mentioned. It is therefore evident that in this royal stele, remarkable for the minuteness of its dates, we have immediately at the commencement to amend another error of the writer, since he had put the first month, Thoth, instead of the second, Phaophi. For, if the error were to be sought in the date of the death-day, and put this a month earlier, we should then have to assume an error in the date of the life-duration, and a double instead of a single one in the number of years since the installation at Memphis.

The Apis of this stele is the same from whose XII. year Dr. Brugsch produces a demotic stele, which fell on the XXXIX. year of Ptolemy IX., Euergetes II., whose birth-day, which previously fluctuated betwixt B.C. 143 and 142, can now be fixed with certainty to the 18th of February, B.C. 142.[85]

It is deserving remark, the official exactness with which, first the date of burial under the *three* Euergetes, then the birth under *two* Euergetes, then again the visit to Nilopolis, the enthronization, and the death under *three* Euergetes, is noted. We learn from it that Euergetes II. put away his wife and sister, Cleopatra II., to marry her daughter, Cleopatra III. ; not, as hitherto assumed from the certainly vague expressions of historians, in the year B.C. 145, but in the course of the XXVIII. or the beginning of the XXIX. year of his reign. In a demotic document of the XXIX. year of his reign, we find already both Cleopatras named ; as upon this stele we find both mentioned in his XXXI. year.

The variations we have just shown for the notices of this stele, from the statements of the historians, are sufficient to raise new doubts against the life-duration attributed by Plutarch to these Apis. And in addition, on two stelæ (Nos. 1904, 1905) of an Apis deceased during the reign of King *Peχi*, it is stated that he had lived 26 years ; another Apis, which died under *Šešonk IV.*, must, according to the computation of stele, No. 1959, have lived longer than 25 years. Mariette (pp. 97—100) concludes, therefore, that if the entire relation of the violent death of Apis be not a fable, that certainly the report of Plutarch of his 25 years must be rejected, and that, perhaps, a life-duration of 28 years should be substituted ; since Osiris, whose living image Apis was, is said by some to have lived or reigned 28 years, and which may have reference, to the sun-cycle of 28 years.

I have, however, shown at an earlier opportunity[86] why we can admit a 28 life-duration neither for Apis nor Osiris, nor was any sun-cycle of 28 years ever used or mentioned by the ancients. It seems that he here means the so-called sun-cycle of 28 years used in the Christian Easter calculations, at the expiration of which, in the Julian Kalendar, the same days of our hebdomadary week fall on the same days of the month. That *such* a cycle could have no significance for the ancient Egyptians, who never had an hebdomadary week, but a decade of ten days, is self-evident. And, on the other hand, it is beyond a doubt that the numerous positive testimonies of Greeks and Romans, on the fixed and impassable term of life assigned to the Apis, could have no foundation. We must, therefore, constantly revert to Plutarch's statement of 25 years, since an error in the MSS. from his mode of expression *cannot* exist, and can find decisive confirmation from the lunar character of Apis in this 25 year moon-period, whose epoch Ptolemy followed throughout an entire Sothic period, and whose multiplication with the Sothic period produced the great Egyptian world-period of 36,525 years.

Reviewing, now, the dates of those Apis-stelæ which offer more precise statements of their life-epoch, we find them as follows :—

Stele No.	Birth in Year	Month	Day	of King	Introduction into Memphis in Year	Month	Day	of King	Death in Year	Month	Day	of King	Burial in Year	Month	Day	of King	Age of Apis Years Mon. Days
1904.	XXVIII.	—	—	*Sesonk III.*	XXVIII. 1. XXIX.	II.	I.	of the same	—	—	—	*Peχi*	II.	VI.	I.	of the same	26. — — dies 25.
1905.	XXVIII.	—	—	*Sesonk III.*	//////////////////////			of the same	—	—	—	*Peχi*	II.	VI.	I.	of the same	26. — — dies 25.
1906.	//////////	—	—	*Sesonk III.*	XXIX.	II.	....	of the same	—	—	—	*Peχi*	////////////////////				— — —
1959.	XI.	—	—	*Sesonk IV.*	XII.	VIII.	IV.	of the same	—	—	—	*Sesonk IV.*	XXXVII.	III.	XXVII.	of the same	— — —
2037.	XXVI.	—	—	*Taharka.*	XXVI.	VIII.	IX.	of the same	XX.	XII.	XX.*	*Psametik I.*	XXI.	II.	XXV.	of the same	— — —
2243.	LIII.	VI.	XIX.	*Psametik I.*	LIV.	III.	XII.	of the same	XVI.	II.	VI.	*Nekau II.*	XVI.	IV.	XVI.	of the same	16. 7. 17. dies 22.
2244.	XVI.	II.	VII.†	*Nekau II.*	I.	XI.	IX.	*Psam. II.*	XII.	VIII.	XII.	*Apries*	XII.	X.	XXI.	of the same	17. 6. 5.
2250.	V.	I.	VII.	*Amasis*	V.	X.	XVIII.	of the same	XXIII.	VII.	VI.	*Amasis*	XXIII.	IX.	XV.	of the same	18. 6. — dies 5. 29.
2284.	V.	V.	XXVII.	*Kambyses*	//////////////////////				IV.	IX.	III.	*Darius*	IV.	XI.	XIII.	of the same	7. 3. 5.
....	XXVIII.	V.	XXIV.	*Ptol. Euerg. II.*	XXXI.	I.	XXIII.	of the same	LI.	XII.	XXII.	*Ptol. Euerg. II.*	LII. 1. II.	I.	XXVII.	of the same	23. 6. 29. dies 28.

* M. de Rougé writes in his table XXI.

† It is remarkable that, from this, this Apis was born on the day immediately following the death of his predecessor. [Note of the Translator.—The reader is referred to a lithograph copy, by Sir Gardner Wilkinson, of some of these stelæ, in the third number of the "Transactions of the Chronological Institute of London;" where No. 2243 is numbered VII. and VIII., 2244 is No. IX., and 2250 No. XII.]

From this table the following general remarks force themselves on our notice. These stelæ are all exact in the mention of the day of *introduction* into the temple of Phtha, at Memphis, and of the day of *burial.* On the contrary, five of these stelæ, and just the five oldest, mention the day of birth with great want of precision, and only for the year; and the four oldest omit the date of death entirely. Exactness in the date of burial is intelligible, because it was also the consecration date of the stelæ. The date of death was 70 days earlier, and could be easily calculated without any express mention. But the proportion of the dates given for the births to those of the installation, proves that the day of the enthronization of Apis was much more important, and more carefully noted than that of his birth. It is evident that the birth-day was not always exactly noted by the older priesthood, and it is evident that if an Apis was not found and recognised immediately after its birth, it might frequently be difficult afterwards to fix exactly the date of that event. It is not, therefore, improbable that the 25 Apis years were counted, not from its uncertain birth, but from the date of its enthronization. The manner in which Plutarch's casual mention of this number is made opposes nothing to such a supposition; still less any of the passages of the ancients bearing upon it. Under this assumption, the dates of the stele, No. 1959, would offer no difficulties. But the 26 years of the earlier Apis rest, in my opinion, upon one of those simple errors of calculation that occur so frequently on other monuments. The XXVIII. year of *Šešonk III.* was taken as the year of Apis birth; but he reigned, not 52 years, only 51. The age of this steer was evidently calculated from his birth-year, and if this is inexact, so also is his age. From XXVIII. to LI. year was cast at 24, or, to the second year of his successor, at 26 years, by including the first and last year in one of the two cases. The so frequent fault of including both first and last day, instead of only one of these two, is just the same as here also in the count of the years, and that this error appears on two stelæ, is thereby explained, that they were set at the same time by the same parties. The stele (pp. 95, 96) given by Mariette seems certainly at variance with this computation; for, when this Apis was brought into Memphis, in XXVIII. years, II. months, and I. day, and was born in the same year, his birth must have happened at the commencement of that year, certainly in its first month; and the result is that more than 25 years elapsed from the enthronization to the death. If, however, the short period of at the utmost 30 days betwixt birth and introduction into the temple, must appear suspicious, since from the historic reports, and other Apis stelæ, more than five months were usually interposed,[87] the stele, No. 1906, referring to the same Apis, proves that another error must be corrected, on the stele, No. 1904, which Mariette alone gives; for in No. 1906 the enthronization is put in the XXIX. year of the king, not in his XXVIII. The average period betwixt birth and enthronization of the following Apis is nine months. If, accordingly, we take that this Apis was born XXVIII. years, V. months, I. day, his life-duration from his birth would be 24 years, 10 months, and 25 days, and from his enthronization 24 years, 1 month, and 20 days. It is not improbable that the priests were allowed to kill the Apis before the total expiration of 25 years, perhaps in the course of the 25th, as M. de Rougé has already surmised; since hitherto no Apis can be pointed out that lived exactly 25 years, whether from birth or installation. Those who are not satisfied with this attempted explanation of the 26 years on the earliest Apis-stele, must believe that Plutarch's statement of 25 years must have been settled in later times, possibly since Psametich I.; a possibility that I took occasion previously to mention. For it must be particularly noted that the more exact statement, as well as entry in the temple registers of these dates, begins only with an Apis born in the LIII. year of Psametich I., as the period in which, according to Mariette, a new large gallery of tombs was constructed, and in which the entire worship of Apis was raised to greater reverence

NOTES.

[1] Monuments of Egypt and Ethiopia, Division III., 246, *b*.

[2] Seconde Lettre au Duc de Blacas, 1826, p. 119, *seqq*.

[3] Monuments, Vol. II., 1833, p. 261, Plate VII.

[4] Egypt's Place in the World's History; Third Book, pp. 121, 133, 136; Plates X., XI. It is an error (if not, perhaps, of the printer) that in p. 135, behind OSERKAN II., we have "Son." The genealogy preceding it at p. 133 gives no such relationship, but places rightly *Osarkon*, as spouse, next *Rakamat*, the daughter of a predecessor, here presumed. Mariette, in his papers on the Apis (Athén. Franç., Bulletin Archéol., 1855, Nov., p. 90), thinks that he ought to conclude from the circumstance that in the above genealogy, *Rakamat* is placed as wife next *Osarkon*, either that my communication to Bunsen was not completed or was not completely given; since it appears, from the vases published by me (Monum., Divis. III., p. 255), the wife of Osarkon II. was called *Hes-en-khev*. He overlooks, however, that my communication to Bunsen in his English edition, merely copied from the German, was made before my journey into Egypt, and before I was acquainted with the vases of H. Campion; and also that *certainly* this *Rakamat* is called, on the Nile statue, the wife of Osarkon, whom he himself takes for Osarkon II.; and therefore that she ought to have been mentioned as the first or second wife of this king, together with *Hes-en-khev*. Nor is his other objection to this genealogy well-founded, that in it Takelot should not have been supposed the son of Scheschonk II., since the direct succession is broken after Scheschonk; on the contrary, the direct succession from father to son, which should always be presumed within the same dynasty, is now supported also by the monuments. The proof is found in the Apis-stele, No. 1898; formerly the connexion, as suggested in the genealogy, could be only presumed. [See the passage subsequently added, and Note (*), p. 16.]

[5] M. de Rougé (*Notice sur quelques Textes Hiéroglyphiques*, p. 33) reads this name, *Pinem*, giving the group, a double reading, *nem*, after Birch, in Bunsen's Engl. Ed., I., p. 565, and *netem* according to group . But the sound, *nem*, is not yet documented by Birch, and the position of the signs in *net-m* points rather to a composition of and . We frequently meet the group ; and this may also be a compound; it seems to me, however, that it is the phonetic sound of as *s*.

[6] I have placed the inscriptions relating hereto together, in the Monuments, Divis. III., pp. 247, 248.

[7] Athén. Franç., 1855; Bull. Archéol., p. 95.

[8] The group, "to his son who loves him (Apis)," or at least the preposition of the dative case, ought to have been repeated.

[9] It also occurs here that the sign [hieroglyph] does not stand before [hieroglyph] but behind it, so that it might as easily be referred to the name of the king, "son of the king, Takelut," as "royal son of Takelut." In the groups, [hieroglyphs] and [hieroglyphs] the sign [hieroglyph] precedes; but in the pronunciation, in all cases, it came last; so that it is only by the genitive particle, which is also frequently wanting in the substantives, that substantive can be distinguished from adjective.

[10] The [hieroglyphs] "Princes of Kush," were not usually sons of kings. But that there can be here no reference is shown by the context of the inscription; even if the group, [hieroglyphs], against the general rule, were wanting.

[10*] In Kahira (Cairo) I obtained a small mummy-statue for the Berlin Museum, which has the same name, with the addition, Mimut, in a royal shield.—Monum. from Egypt, Divis. III., 256, *d*.

[11] We certainly know, besides the two Osarkons of the Dynasty, also a third Osarkon; but, as this name, however, recurs in the XXIII. Dynasty, one of these three Osarkons is to be attributed to this Dynasty.

[11*] Monum. Divis. III., 254, *c*. Champollion, in his "Lettres," p. 190, gives the 22nd year from Selseleh, and from him it has passed into Bunsen's and other books. But the date ought to be referred to the above-mentioned Stele, which only gives the 21st year.

[12] Wilkinson, Mat. Hierogl., P. II., Pl. II., gives this king from the monuments an eleventh regnal year. I know no such date; Wilkinson seems to have confounded him with Takelut II., whose eleventh year is found twice at Karnak. Mon., Div. III., 255, *i*, 257, *a*.

[13] Mon., Div. III., 257, *a*.

[14] Mon., Div. III., 256, *a*.

[15] Not on this but on another Apis-stele, No. 1904, is the same *Tesbastperu* called *Princess*. The reading, *bast*, for [hieroglyph] was first placed by Mariette beyond doubt.

[16] But Mariette, also, in a note (No. 17) to his "Tableau Généalogique," adduces the possibility of the identity of King Takelut with an officer of the same name.

[17] Mariette adduces, in his Genealogical Table, and p. 94, only one wife, *Taari*, and calls her also sister: this last statement is certainly not to be read on my copy of this somewhat mutilated stele. All three sons, however, were from different wives. Instead of [hieroglyphs] Mariette might possibly have more correctly read [hieroglyphs] "*Tatitaneb*."

[18] Mon., Div. III., 255, *e-h*.

[19] We have remarked above that this *Namurot* is called, not "Prince," but only "Son," of King *Osarkon*. It is possible that the former title is not given him because *Namurot* was born prior to Osarkon becoming king.

[20] Champollion, "Lettre au Duc de Blacas," II., p. 125, knew only the Turin fragment.

[21] Egyptian Inscriptions, I., p. 35, *A*.

[22] [hieroglyphs] can have another meaning. This title is, however, regularly given only to the sons or daughters of princes.

[23] Pl. 137.

[24] Selection of the Principal Documents of Ægypt. Antiq., Plate XV.

[25] But the determinative of the word, [hieroglyph] "the Lord," bears in the second line of the back inscription the Uræus, [hieroglyph].

[26] It is, namely from the pontiff title of *Menχeperra* himself, very probable that he was the son of the first, not of the second Pisem, who had already perfect royal shields.

[27] Burton, Exc. Hierogl., Pl. XL., found in Tanis inscriptions of the XII. Dynasty, which I sought in vain. Their presence would carry back the royal buildings, and the first foundation of the temple, at least to that latest Dynasty of the Old Kingdom.

[28] The portion of the statue wanting is said to have been carried away by Rifaud. Burton, Exc. Hierogl., Pl. XL., saw also the inscription in the same mutilated state as myself.

[29] Transact. of the Roy. Soc. of Lit., Second Series, Vol. III., p. 165, *seqq*.

[30] "I have entered into this philological detail because I think it demonstrates, by a new route, an alliance between the Assyrian and Egyptian courts, and shows that at the period connexions of blood must have existed between the two royal houses."

[31] Mariette, Bull. Archéol., 1855, p. 97.

[32] 1 Kings, iii. 1.

[33] Syncellus, p. 184, *A*. 'Ο δὲ ('Ιεροβωάμ) προσφυγὼν τῷ Σουσακεὶμ βασιλεῖ Αἰγύπτου γαμβρὸς αὐτοῦ γίνεται ἐπὶ θυγατρί. *Boeckh* (Manetho, p. 315), and from him Birch (l. l., p. 166), call her a "sister" of the king.

[34] On Monuments, Div. III., 196, the form of this cap is correctly represented; it differs from the common head-dress of *χeta*, as represented in the battles, but calls to mind the caps on the Assyrian monuments. The slight variation from them may be put down to the want of exactness by the Egyptian hierogrammist in his delineation.

[35] *Prisse*, Monum., Pl. XXIV. *Birch*, Transact. of the Roy. Soc. of Literature, Vol. IV., 2nd Series, p. 217, *seqq*.

[36] Mariette reads *Teh-en-buiua*, and adds the preceding group, *Tehen*, to the name; but, since it has an hieroglyphic determinative, there may rather be in it a title, or other personal distinction. The *n* cannot be separated from *teh*, since [hieroglyph] appears sometimes alone, sometimes as determinative behind the group, *tehen*, for which, occasionally, certainly only *teh* is written (see the variations in Goldhornames of Amenophis III.; Sharpe, Egypt. Mon., 2nd Series, Pl. 92, 1). The two last signs, [hieroglyph] usually denote a repetition of the preceding word, or of a portion of it; we therefore differ. The group, [hieroglyph] *χenen*, which precedes most of the private names of men and of one woman in this genealogy, Mariette renders, I conceive, by a happy supposition, as "du même rang."

[37] Rosellini, Vol. II., p. 88, Wiener Realwörterb. s. v. Zerach. Birch, l. l., p. 167, and others. But see, *per contra*, Ewald, "Gesch. des Volks Isr.," 2nd Edition, III., p. 470. Thenius zur Chron., 14, 8; Bunsen, and others.

[38] Remarkable is, however, in this name, the ideographic sign, [hieroglyph] the sound of which, *šu*, has not yet been placed beyond doubt.

[39] The tom-cat is generally called [hieroglyphs] (Todtenbuch, c. xvii. 45, 46, 47, cxxv. 40) Copt. ϢⲀⲨ ; and [hieroglyphs] the she-cat (Champ. Gramm., p. 72): but *šau* reciprocates with *ši*; e.g. in the great papyrus of the dead at Paris, c. cxxv. 40.

[40] Eusebius gives the true designation, but omits the names of the V. Dynasty. Africanus changes erroneously the designations of the V. and VI. Dynasty; he should call that Memphitic and this Elephantine.

[40*] Herod., IV. 180.

[41] The name [hieroglyphs] *Bekenranf*, first found out by Mariette, was by him referred, with great probability, to King Βόκχορις (Βόχχορις) of Grecian writers. The name was previously known as that of a private person, under Psametich I., from a large rock sepulchral chamber at Saqara, whose possessor may have been a descendant of King Bocchoris. The separate parts of the names are easily reducible to Egyptian words, and of the single signs [hieroglyph] is not in the most common Egyptian phonetic alphabet. It certainly belongs to a row of other signs, [hieroglyphs], which admit, sooner than others, in foreign names, pure phonetic meanings, in place of their original ideographic character. These are, nearly all, merely such signs as whose consonant sounds are followed by only a single vowel, with which it formed an entire word, and therefore frequently the stroke ǀ is added; as, [hieroglyph] *si*, [hieroglyph] *sa*, [hieroglyph] *ro*, [hieroglyph] *la*, [hieroglyph] *ka*, [hieroglyph] *ba*. To these belongs also [hieroglyphs], which, in proper names, commonly loses its signification as an interjection, Copt. ω. Still, the name, *Bekenranf*, has too much of Egyptian stamp to admit my viewing it as foreign.

[41*] Chronol. der Ægypt. p. 313: "Manetho gives, in the XXVI. Dynasty, three "direct ancestors of Psametich, who, contrary to the general opinion hitherto, did not "live *after* the Æthiopians, but *contemporaneously* with them. This being contempo-"raneous is already noticed by Eusebius, and we shall revert to it below. Even "occasional allusions in Herodotus point to it, since (II. 152) he says that Sabakôs "persecuted *Psametich* earlier than the Dodecarchy, and drove him into Syria, and that "the same Ethiopian had killed the father of Psametich Nekôs (that is, Nechao I. of "Manetho). The Ethiopic Dynasty of Manetho is there only a *side dynasty*."

[42] Notice de quelques Textes Hiéroglyphiques, publiés par M. Greene, p. 40.

[43] Acad. Monthly Report (Berl.), 1854, August.

[44] Transact. of Germ. Eastern Soc., 1853, p. 422. Acad. Monthly Report, 1854, August, p. 495, *seqq*.

[45] On the assumption of the year 525, the conquest falls in the *fifth*, not in the *third* year of the Persian reign of Cambyses, and when M. de Rougé says, p. 39, "Si nous plaçons maintenant, avec les meilleures autorités, la conquête de l'Egypte à la troisième année de Cambyse," etc., it must be, on the contrary, remarked that the *third* is mentioned neither by Africanus, nor by Eusebius, nor by any other authority, but that both in accordance, as well as Syncellus, mention the *fifth* year.

[46] Monthly Report (Berl. Acad.), 1854, p. 497.

[47] It might be doubtful whether one of the four strokes which are joined to the sun's disc belongs to it, or to the number. In the last improbable case, 69 days only are reckoned from the day of death to that of burial, or if both be counted, 70, a mode of

counting found on other stelæ. The mention of the day of burial recurs again on the stelæ, 2285, 2286, 2287, and 2289; but so that in many of these legends the designation of the month is not quite correct.

[48] See at the conclusion of the Paper.

[49] On an Egyptian Stele. Transact. of the R. Irish Academy, Vol. XIX., Pl. II.

[50] See my Paper on a knowledge of the Ptolemaic Hist. in Transact. of Roy. Acad. of Sciences, 1852, p. 484.

[51] According to Aucher, I., p. 220.

[52] From the circumstance that Dr. Hincks did not know my correction of August, 1854, also arises that, in his paper, p. 424, he mentions my assent to the year 527.

[53] A third frequent title of these women must still be different from ; as I have found both used for the same person.

[54] This is the more correct orthography than Amenitis, since the analogous name, is also written .

[55] In Hamamât is wrongly written for . This shield is also found on many stamps in the Berlin and British Museums, as well as, finally, on a scarabæus at Leyden.

[56] I read *Šepuntepu* (without being sure of the interpretation for) as long as no other sound is beyond doubt. The variation is not yet proven for the sound, *ap*, since is well known to stand as phonetic amplification, like in , , , , , &c. There is also difficulty in writing *u* for ×.

[57] M. de Rougé, Not. de qu. Text. Hiérogl., p. 43, transfers this error to Champollion and Rosellini, whilst I alone am responsible for it.

[58] See my Chronol., I., 423.

[59] The throne-shield of Psametich I., formerly read *Ra-ha-het*, I now, after the example of others, based, certainly, only on Manetho's original Οὔαφρις, read, *Uahprahet.* Hincks (Transact. of the R. I. Academy) considers it a *lapsus calami*, or a press error, that I (Month. Rep. of the Berl. Acad., 1853, p. 744) give a 22nd year to "Apries." He has, however, momentarily overlooked that Psametich, to whom alone I allude in this passage, has the same name in his throne-shield, which Apries afterwards assumed, as second shield-name, and that I called Psametich I. by his shield-name, expressly for the sake of perspicuity, and to distinguish him fully from Psametich II., with whom he had formerly been confounded.

[60] The lock, a characteristic mark of children, alternates with *šere*, child, as already remarked by Prisse (Mon. p. 6, to Pl. XXVI.). Compare Rosellini, Mon. di Culto, Tav. XLVII., XLVIII.

[61] Revue Archéol., IV., 625.

[62] Hincks, Chron. of the XXVI. Dynasty, p. 431, makes *Taχot* a daughter of Psametich I. and of *Šepuntepu*, without assigning a reason, but which may have scarcely arisen from a misunderstanding of the sarcophagus. *Vide infra.*

[63] In the original, both this shield and the two following ones have small added cognomens, which are not given here.

[64] And so already before him, Birch, Rev. Arch. IV., 625.

[65] It must be thus read, instead of [hieroglyphs] as it stands in the original.

[66] Leemans (Lettre à Salv., p. 124) has already correctly noted the difference of these two places, and given the opinion that in the first place [hieroglyph] for [hieroglyph] ought to be read. But he imagines Psametich for a son of Nitocris, and her as a daughter of Taχot. Rosellini (Mon. dell' Eg. Text., Vol. VIII., pp. 189, 190) agrees with him.

[67] Chronol., I., 303, 308.

[68] Transact. of the R. Ir. Academy, Vol. XXII., Nov. 1854, p. 436.

[69] Rev. Arch. IV. 625. He was led wrong herein from a faulty reading by G. Harris, who thought he had discovered Anχnes-Ranofrehet as wife, [hieroglyphs] instead of daughter, [hieroglyphs] of Psametich.

[70] Rev. Archéol., IV., 624.

[71] Rev. Archéol., Vol. IV., 123.

[71*] Mon. III., 91.

[72] Sharpe, Eg. Inscr. I., 96.

[73] The reading [hieroglyphs] as given by De Rougé, I have never met with, and it ought to be subsequently verified more exactly.

[74] Leemans, Lettre à Salv., Pl. XXV.

[75] Monum., III., 62, *a*.

[76] Stele at Vienna.

[77] Monum., III., 273, 274.

[78] Champoll., Notices, p. 552.

[79] Ptol. IX., Euergetes II., and Cleopatra II., his first wife, were children of Ptol. V., Epiphanes, and Cleopatra I. Therefore Cleopatra III. is here passed over.

[80] The hieroglyphical text is somewhat more expanded here, but not in every particular intelligible to me.

[81] The original has [hieroglyphs], instead of which, possibly, [hieroglyphs] ought to be read.

[82] Λευκὸν τεῖχος, the white fort or tower; thus was named the strongest portion of Memphis, in which Inaros held himself against the Persians (Thucydides, I., 104). Here, doubtless, was situated the royal castle (from whose high and glittering buildings that quarter may have had its name), as well as the great Phtha-temple: it was, therefore, that portion of the town still remarkable by its high heaps of rubbish, and by its ruins. The castle itself must be sought in the highest pile of ruins, N.E. of Mitrahenneh (marked on the plan of the Prussian expedition, Monum., I., 9, with *A*), which is exactly located, and abutted northwards on the temple of Phthah.

[83] The somewhat indistinct group of the town could be taken for [hieroglyphs], but appears to have been different.

[84] Some other smaller errors are ascribable to the writer, which, as unimportant, I pass by. Egyptian exactness in their inscriptions is never very remarkable.

[85] When I formerly placed the epoch of this Apis conditionally, as the direct proof was wanting, the reason for my doubt was, some time back, retracted (Monthly Report, 1854, p. 222, Note). In like manner, the reason ceases with the regular return of the Apis-periods, for preferring the later years to the earliest, amongst the five birth-

notices of the following Apis (Monthly Report, 1853, p. 740) which falls B.C. 118-7, and which now appears the most probable from our stele.

[6] Acad. Monthly Report, 1854, May, p. 220, *seqq*.

[7] When M. de Rougé, on the Tableau of his treatise, Note 2, reckons the age of a calf brought to Memphis at only four months, his calculation is faulty; for, from his own showing, this Apis was born, 7 Phaophi (II. month); brought in, 9 Phamenoth (VII. month); and in this interval we have, not four, but five months, two days. But the second date is, in the original, not 9 Phamenoth (VII. month), but 9 Epiphi (XI. month); there lie, therefore, nine months and two days betwixt birth and introduction.

THE END.

J. HADDON, PRINTER, CASTLE STREET, FINSBURY.

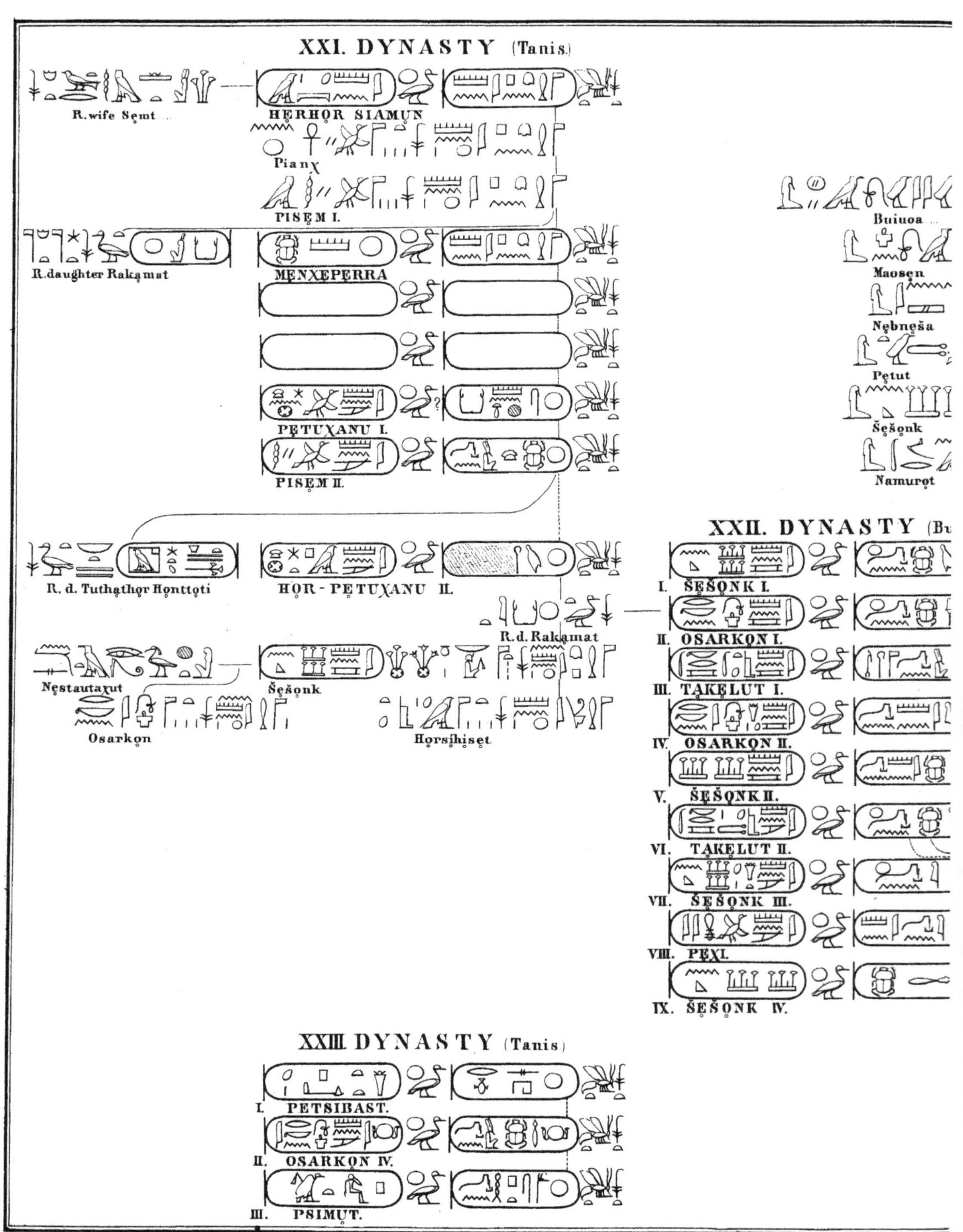
XXI. DYNASTY (Tanis.)
R. wife Semt...
HERHOR SIAMUN
Pianχ
PISEM I.
R. daughter Rakamat
MENXEPERRA
PETUχANU I.
PISEM II.
R. d. Tuthathor Honttoti
HOR-PETUχANU II.
R. d. Rakamat
Nestautaχut
Šešonk
Osarkon
Horsihiset
Buiuoa...
Maosen
Nebneša
Petut
Šešonk
Namurot
XXII. DYNASTY (Bu
I. ŠEŠONK I.
II. OSARKON I.
III. TAKELUT I.
IV. OSARKON II.
V. ŠEŠONK II.
VI. TAKELUT II.
VII. ŠEŠONK III.
VIII. PEχI.
IX. ŠEŠONK IV.
XXIII. DYNASTY (Tanis)
I. PETSIBAST.
II. OSARKON IV.
III. PSIMUT.

Lith. von E. Weidenbach.

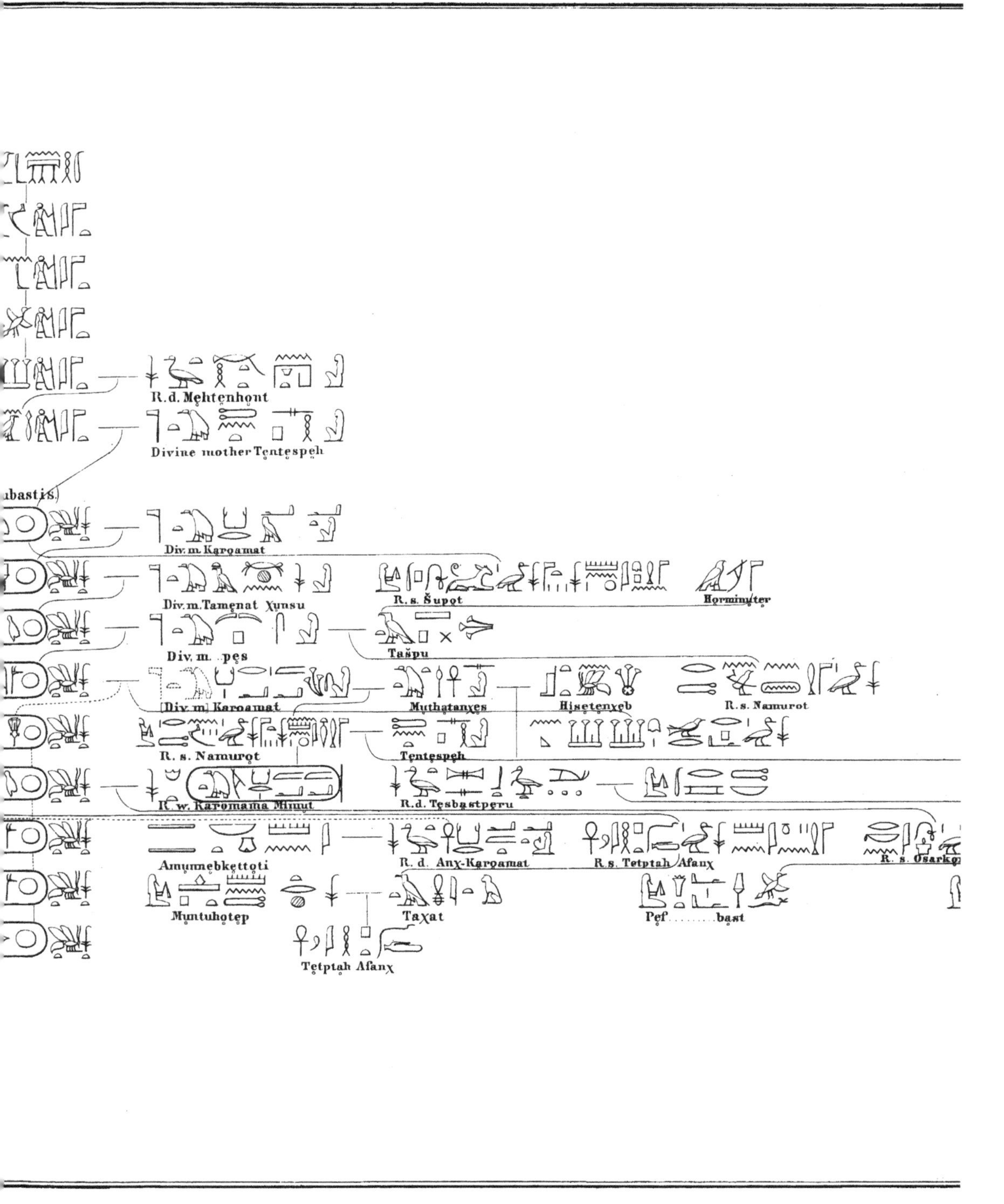

R.d. Meḥtenḥont
Divine mother Teṇteṣpeḥ
ubastis.)
Div. m. Karoamat
Div. m. Tamenat Xunsu
R. s. Šupot
Horminuter
Div. m. ..pes
Tašpu
[Div. m.] Karoamat
Muthatanxes
Hisetenxeb
R. s. Namurot
R. s. Namurot
Teṇteṣpeḥ
R. w. Karomama Mimut
R. d. Teṣbastperu
Amunnebkettoti
R. d. Anx-Karoamat
R. s. Tetptah Afanx
R. s. Osarkọ
Muntuhotep
Taxat
Pef.........bast
Tetptah Afanx

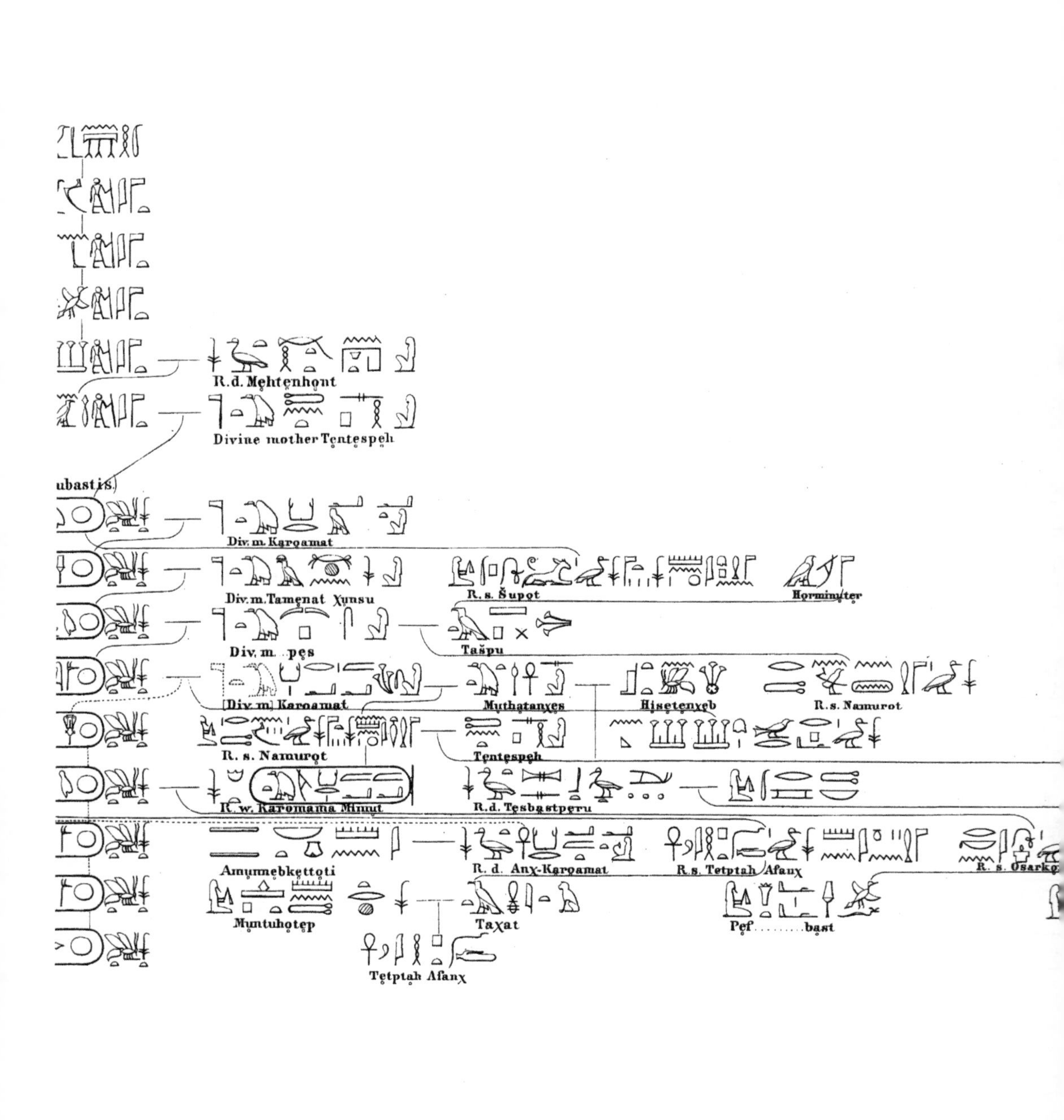

R.d. Mehtenhont
Divine mother Tentespeh
ubastis.)
Div. m. Karoamat
Div. m. Tamenat Xunsu
R. s. Šupot
Horminuter
Div. m. .. pes
Tašpu
[Div. m.] Karoamat
Muthatanxes
Hisetenxeb
R. s. Namurot
R. s. Namurot
Tentespeh
R. w. Karomama Minut
R. d. Tesbastperu
Amunnebkettoti
R. d. Anx-Karoamat
R. s. Tetptah Afanx
R. s. Osarko
Muntuhotep
Taxat
Pef.........bast
Tetptah Afanx

R.d. Tentespeh

Pethiset — Taari — ....her.... — ....irit — Honptah

Takelut — Horsihiset — Muttithor — Hapushiset — Pesonhor — Petpettitis

Takelut — Anx-Pethiset — Honptah — Irituru

Pesonhor

Lith. Inst v. C. Monecke in Berlin.

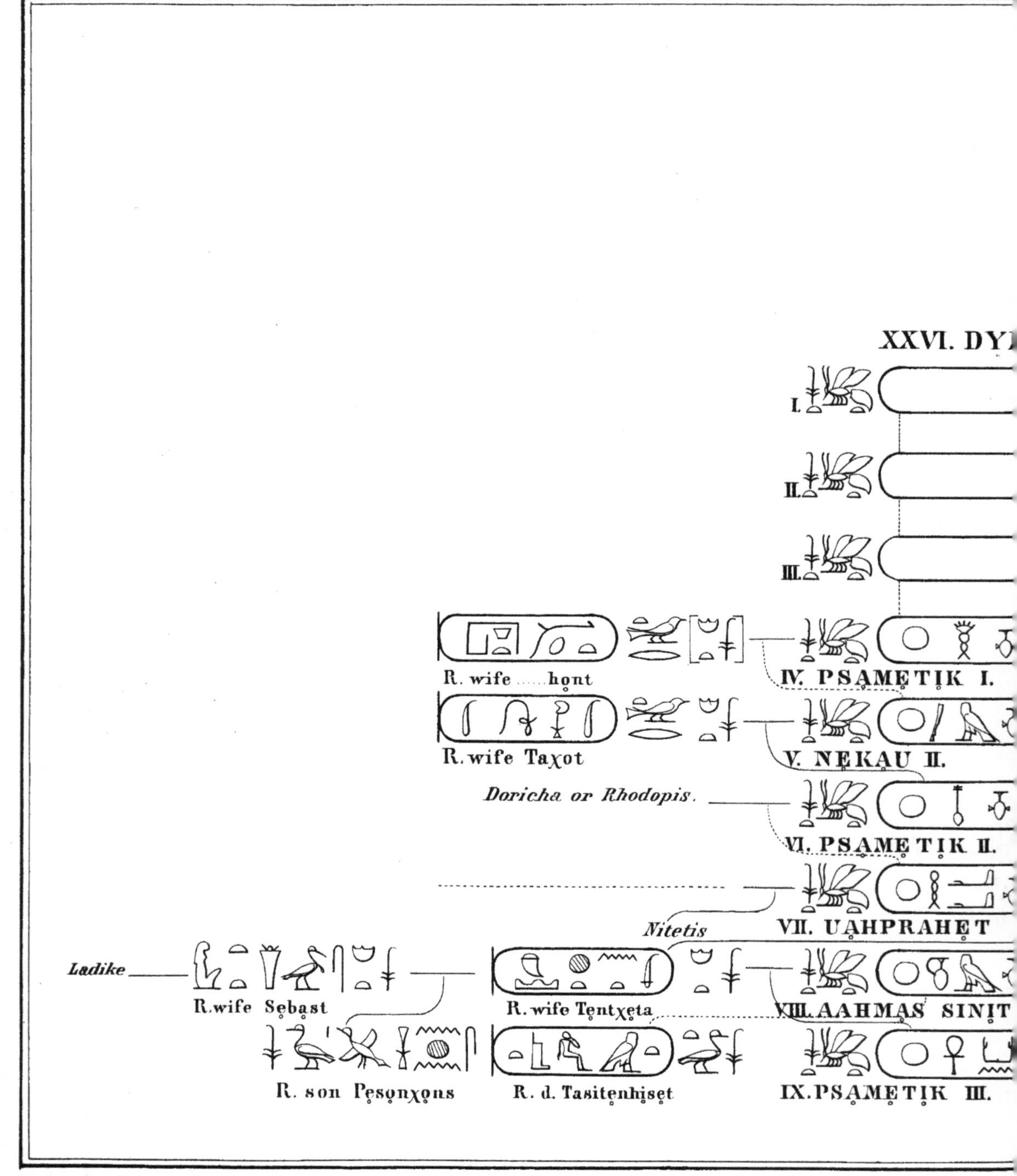

Lith. von E. Weidenbach.

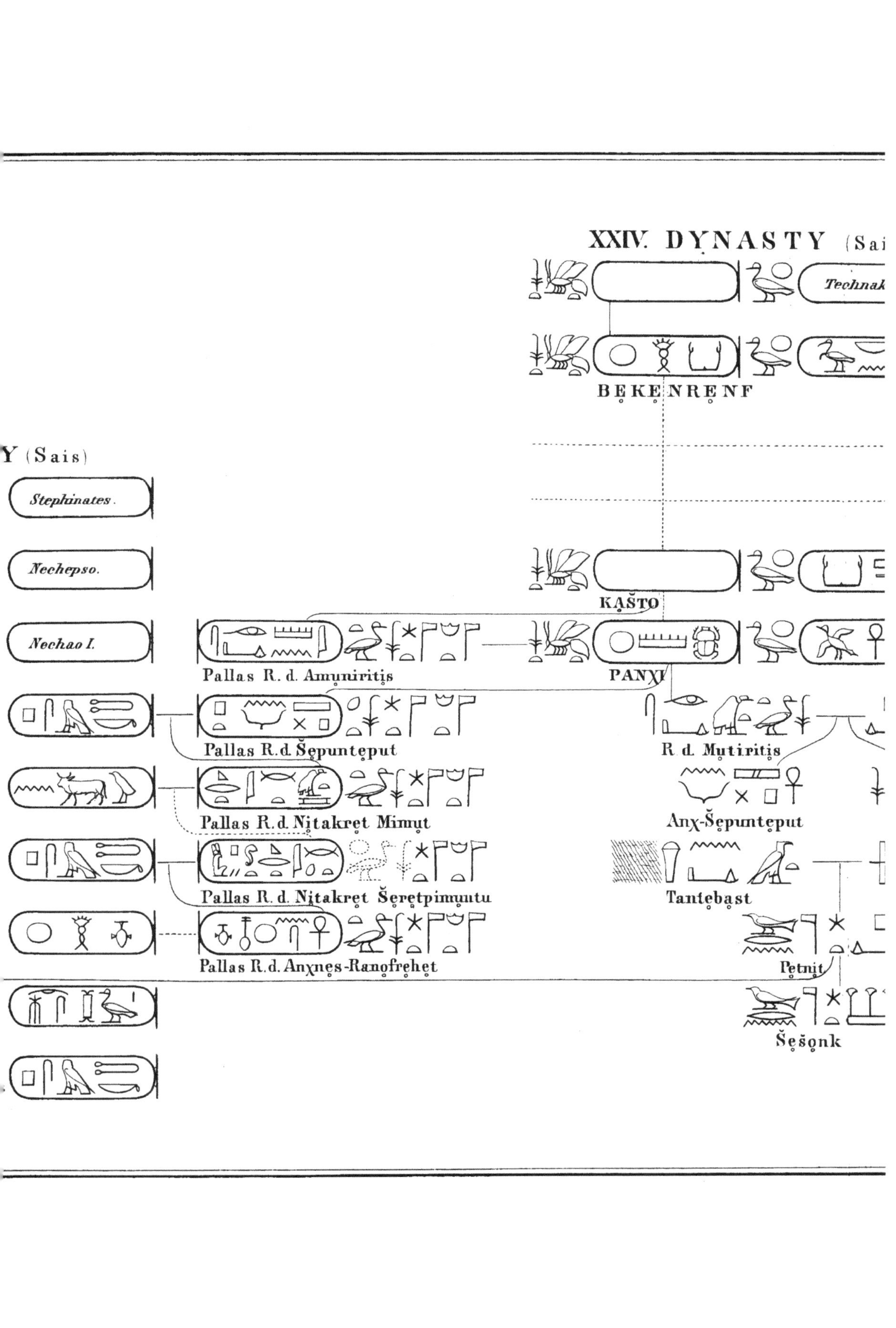
XXIV. DYNASTY (Sai
Y (Sais)
Stephinates.
Nechepso.
Nechao I.
Technak
BEKENRENF
KAŠTO
PANXI
Pallas R. d. Amuniritis
Pallas R.d. Šepunteput
Pallas R.d. Nitakret Mimut
Pallas R. d. Nitakret Šeretpimuntu
Pallas R.d. Anxnes-Ranofrehet
R. d. Mutiritis
Anx-Šepunteput
Tantebast
Petnit
Šešonk

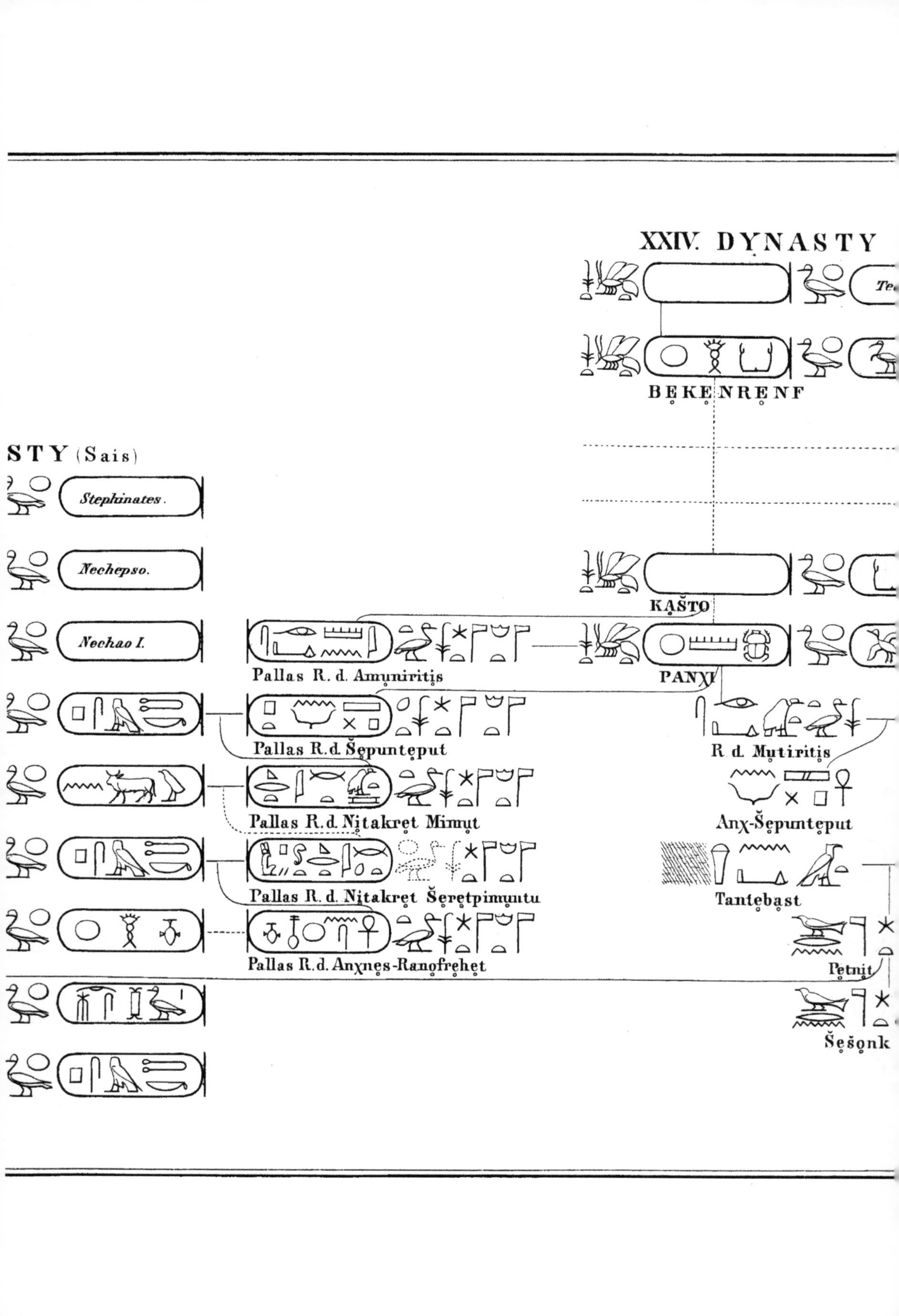
XXIV. DYNASTY
BEKENRENF
KAŠTO
PANXI
R. d. Mutiritis
Anχ-Šepunteput
Tantebast
Petnit
Šešonk
STY (Sais)
Stephinates.
Nechepso.
Nechao I.
Pallas R. d. Amuniritis
Pallas R. d. Šepunteput
Pallas R. d. Nitakret Mimut
Pallas R. d. Nitakret Šeretpimuntu
Pallas R. d. Anχnes-Ranofrehet

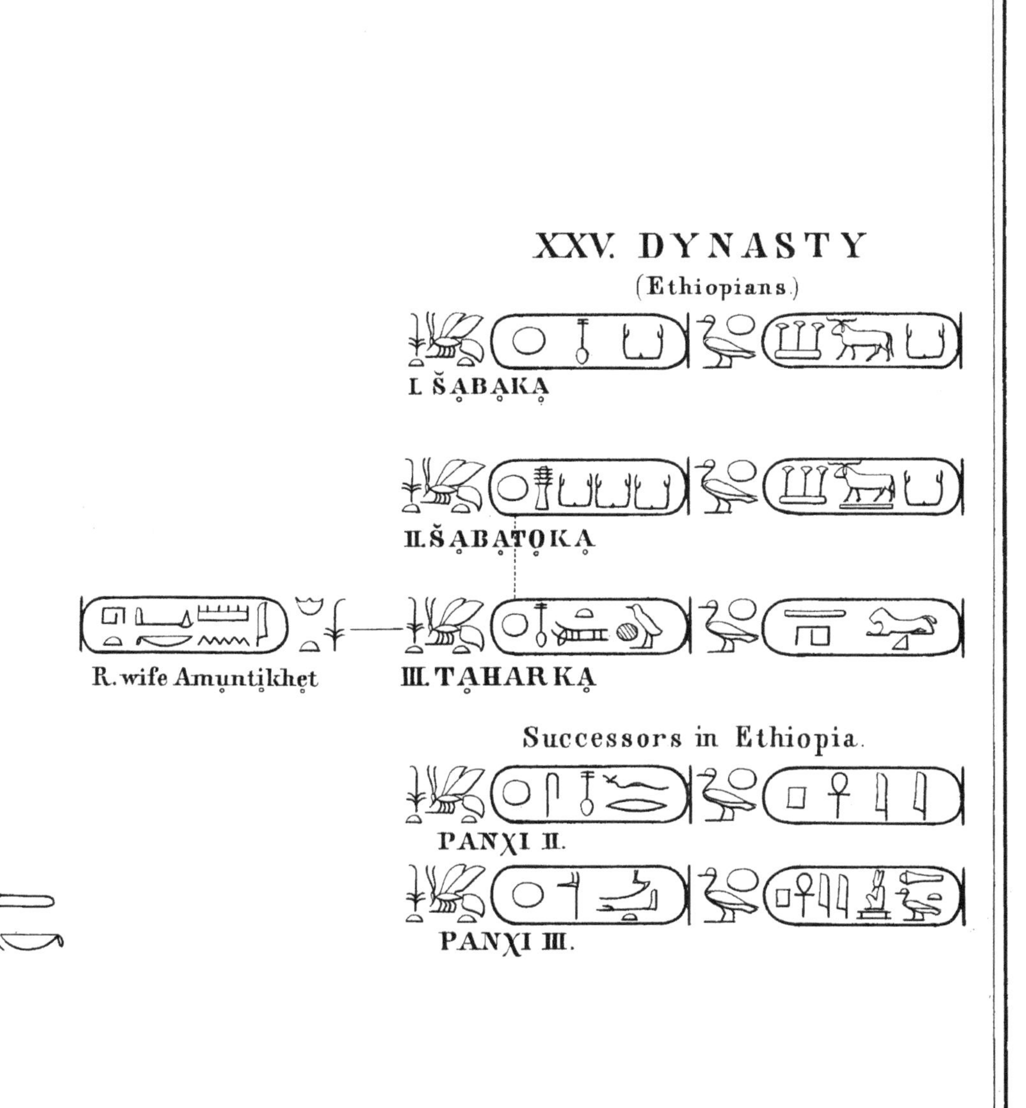

Lith. Inst. v. C. Monecke in Berlin.

www.ingramcontent.com/pod-product-compliance
Ingram Content Group UK Ltd.
Pitfield, Milton Keynes, MK11 3LW, UK
UKHW030902150625
459647UK00021B/2654